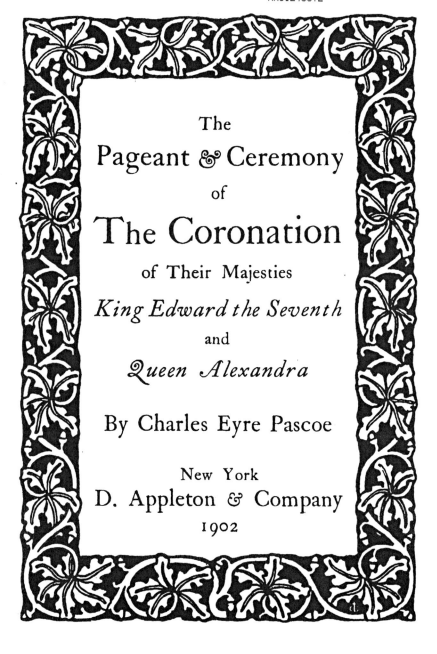

The

Pageant & Ceremony

of

The Coronation

of Their Majesties

King Edward the Seventh

and

Queen Alexandra

By Charles Eyre Pascoe

New York

D. Appleton & Company

1902

Crowns and Coronets of England

CONTENTS

PART I

THE ACCESSION, PROCLAMATION, AND MEET-ING OF THE FIRST PARLIAMENT OF KING EDWARD THE SEVENTH

Contents

6

Contents

PART IV

THE AUTHOR'S PREFACE

"FOR NOW SITS EXPECTATION IN THE AIR"

THE Author of this book or compilation (as the critical shall decide) must be allowed to be exceptionally favoured, in that he has found an American constituency, no less than one nearer home, not unwilling to consider what he may herein have to say. All the more contented should he be, with this promising prospect of a co-partnership of interest in his work, since he knows from previous experiences in journalism and pencraft, that he has nothing but the fullest measure of generosity and kindness to expect from one party at least to this arrangement—the American Reader, namely. "They" (the Americans) "are the most genial people on the face of the earth," as his Excellency the British Ambassador in Washington (Lord Pauncefote) has recently reminded us *— if any of us need to be reminded: "At the first

---

* The *Times*, July 19th, 1901.

The Coronation of Edward VII

grip of the hand they take you to their hearts. So long as you do not try to deal underhand with them, so long as you do not assume superior airs they treat you as one of their own ; and who can say more?" None, indeed, can say more; and what is so said is worthily and truly said, by an English nobleman who, by reason of his exalted station as representative of his country in the United States, should know and understand Americans better than the majority.

An American, when you get to know him, generally turns out to be a not very distant kinsman of an Englishman. Ought we not more properly to write Britisher, or Briton? except that the euphony of neither word seems somehow or other so pleasing and inviting, to one who is English born himself, as the designation he so greatly cherishes, and for which he seeks precedence and publicity whenever and wherever he finds opportunity. An American (needless to repeat) generally turns out to be a not very distant kinsman of one whose people, or ancestors, are English, Scotch, or Irish born ; which doubtless serves better. For the which reason, the Author ventures upon the liberty of asking his Readers to accept of this

The Author's Preface

prefatory chapter as being addressed indiscriminately to each, either, or all four. The Englishman who reads it cannot possibly object to being included in the company of the most agreeable, generous, and hospitable of his kinsmen across the seas. The Scotchman can find nothing but satisfaction in having his nationality thus promptly and spontaneously recognised as British by an Englishman. The Irishman will at once see the humour in this particular instance of our trying to save trouble, in making one preface serve the purposes of four. Finally, the American may possibly concede that we must be much more clever than, perchance, he believes us to be, if we succeed in pleasing any.

*   *   *   *   *

No author, in our opinion, can hope to establish himself in the friendly consideration of his Reader, until he makes some sort of overtures to that end. He may hope soonest to gain that most valuable auxiliary in his work by dropping all appearance of pretension and artificiality at the outset, and discovering himself, so to say, as he really is: "This is the man you are talking with." "No

The Coronation of Edward VII

man living is free from speaking foolish things "—
as a wise and experienced philosopher has truly
said : " the ill-luck is to speak them curiously."

> ' This fellow sure with much ado,
> Will tell great tales and trifles too.'

" That concerneth not me," he adds ". . . I do
but buy or sell mine for what they weigh.   I
speak unto paper as to the first man I meet."

The use of the personal pronoun in print does
not necessarily imply that the user is inclined
to be vain and consequential.   It far more often
means that he is the very reverse of presuming,
and much more disposed to plainness and modesty.
He places himself, as it were, in the opposite chair
to his Reader, and invites him on equal terms to
conversation.   The style of the impersonal or
editorial "we" is far more pretentious, tending
to make an author conceited with himself, and
pompous and pragmatical towards his Reader.
Writing is but another name for conversation, and
whether one write well or ill, has anything new
to relate, or nothing new to relate, depend upon
it he will be in a better position to deserve
the Reader's attention if he show some spirit of

The Author's Preface

cordiality, tapping him on the coat-sleeve, as it were, in friendly and companionable manner, rather than if he adopt the more reserved attitude, merely exhibiting the customary courtesy of the hat, and indulging in a few commonplace compliments. There are some, of course, who would resent the slightest indication of the raising of the forefinger to the coat-sleeve, by way of opening a casual conversation. But let such persons pass. We have no sort of desire to intrude either upon their exclusiveness or their pride.

He who would have friends must show himself friendly. None of us can afford to do without them. I know of no better way of attempting to make friends in a book, than by seeking a cordial good understanding with your Reader in the very first paragraph you write. Your purpose, you tell him, is only a little haphazard talk about this matter or that; and if he find anything interesting, or agreeable, in the conversation, so much the pleasanter for both. So, let's to our respective armchairs—you in this, and I in that, and see if it be not possible to bring about a little mutual goodwill, and—may we not hope?—mutual appreciation, if not forbearance, without insisting on the

The Coronation of Edward VII

preliminary formality of a too ceremonious introduction.

I never yet knew an American who thought any the worse of an Englishman, because he divested himself of all airs and pretensions, and sought to gain his goodwill by such friendly overtures as I propose. Nor are Englishmen in the aggregate so churlish and uncivil as to reject the offer of a stranger's acquaintance if he do not presume to demand too much consideration at their hands.

At a first glance at its title-page, it might seem as if this book could have but slight interest for American Readers. The Pageant and Ceremony of a Coronation provides but scanty fare for the many who cannot have the opportunity of being spectators of either. For those Americans who propose to see both, this book will be found to furnish forth, I think, a sufficient meal. The cynically inclined, perchance, might find in its contents somewhat that lends point to an observation to be found in Johnson's "Life of Milton," that "the trappings of Monarchy (namely) would set up an ordinary commonwealth." However that may be, none can say that the author has willingly wandered into the thorny and uninviting field of politics. This book will be found much

14

The Author's Preface

more historical than political, and more gossipy and discursive, perhaps, than either. Of course, it keeps well in view the Present Interest belonging to its subject. That, in point of fact, as every one will see, is its *raison d'être*.

    *   *   *   *   *

England is so near to America nowadays, happily in more senses than one, that the sights, attractions, pastimes, and amusements of the one country are become almost part and parcel of the sights, attractions, pastimes, and amusements of the other. There is, however, one sight which occurs only once or possibly twice in a lifetime, which America has not yet succeeded in reproducing, and never will succeed in reproducing, and that sight is a Coronation in Westminster Abbey! I am much mistaken, if some Americans are not sufficiently interested as to desire to know how that ceremony is nowadays performed. This book will tell them. The necessities of the case require that it should dip a little into History; but if "History is" (as Henry St. John, Lord Bolingbroke, said) "Philosophy teaching by examples," I greatly misjudge my American Readers if they hastily throw it aside because it in some

measure discusses matters in which they find but
little interest. The history of the one country up
to a point is the history of the other, and it may be,
in time to come—who dares venture to prophesy ?—
that eventful and splendid history may be yet more
closely interwoven and become the common stock
of both countries again. Perhaps one likes to dream
so. If Americans might only be brought to believe
it, there are no people in the world more generously
thought of by Englishmen than they, nor are there
any they so willingly form friendships with at home
or abroad. The one regret that most of us, who
visit America, feel on leaving its shores, is that we
are so seldom able to repay in full measure the
hospitality and kindness shown to us while staying
in that country.

In bringing this already too lengthy opening
chapter to a close, I venture to quote a passage
from the published speeches, if I remember aright,
of the late Mr. Phelps, sometime American Ambassador to England, which I read lately, seated
in the pleasant reading-room of the St. Botolph Club
in Boston ; a club which has ever shown in largest
measure hospitality and kindness to Englishmen.
" The time is long past " (thus the record) " when kings

The Author's Preface

and rulers can involve their nations in hostilities to gratify their own ambitions or caprice. There can be no war nowadays between civilised nations, nor any peace that is not hollow or delusive, unless sustained and backed up by the sentiment of the people who are parties to it. Before nations can quarrel, their inhabitants must first become hostile. Then a cause of quarrel is not far to seek. There are no dragon's teeth so prolific as mutual misunderstanding. . . . It is in the great and constantly increasing intercourse between England and America, in its reciprocities and amenities, that the security against misunderstanding must be found. While that continues, the relations between the two countries cannot be otherwise than friendly." That the intercourse between England and America is happily yearly increasing, and is destined to increase in far greater measure as the years pass on, there cannot be a shadow of doubt. God grant that the concord and amity of the two nations in time to come may be such as to entitle the twain to the proud designation of States united.

Points about Pedigrees

MIGHT it not be well sometimes if we were not to take the things of the world too seriously? Cheerfulness is ever better than dulness; and, truly, much melancholy is a weariness of the flesh. "Though David's son, the sad and splendid," declared mourning to be better than feasting; we shall maintain to the contrary, yea, though even all the kings of the earth were to rise in opposition. Methinks that London will lose somewhat of mirth and gladness, for example, in being deprived of its historic Coronation banquet in Westminster Hall. But that's a matter for his Majesty the King's decision, not to be impertinently discussed by a mere subject. "Health at

Points about Pedigrees

your bidding serve your Majesty!" and let all the people shout, "God save the King!"

Sterne it was, if I am not mistaken—I think I have somewhere read a sermon of his preached in the Minster of York, whereof he was, as most of us know, some time Prebendary, touching on this very topic: Sterne it was who was firmly persuaded that every time a man smiles, but much more so when he laughs, it adds somewhat to whatever fragment of life—more or less as the years speed by—may be permitted him. Far be it from the compiler of these pages to smile inopportunely. There is to everything a season, and a time to every purpose under heaven. This is serious matter we are now occupied upon. And so were the Barons occupied with serious matter the other day, when on being directed by Norroy King of Arms to pass out of the House of Lords into the Royal Gallery, "two and two, in order of precedence," some of their lordships not merely smiled, but laughed *—with no derogation of personal dignity, it may be hoped, as peers of the realm, or of collective dignity as judges, specially summoned to

* Case of Earl Russell, tried in the Royal Gallery of the House of Lords. *Times* report, July 19th, 1901.

The Coronation of Edward VII

a solemn trial of one of their order. Some of their lordships laughed. It being a very hot July day, inviting to slumber, they were taken unawares (so to say) by the mandate of Norroy King of Arms; were not quite certain of themselves for the moment—

> "Are we lords?
> Or do we dream, or have we dream'd till now?
> We do not sleep: we see, we hear, we speak.
>
> *   *   *   *   *   *   *
>
> My lords, they say that we have dream'd,
> And slept above six hundred years, or more."

This present being the year of grace 1902, second of the reign of his Most Gracious Majesty King Edward the Seventh (whom God preserve!) some of us are not prepared to be suddenly transported back to the times of the Plantagenets, to the times (let's say) of that High and Mighty Prince, Edward the Third, of Glorious Memory. Like little children on being awakened out of a sleep, we smile. But 'tis a pleasant good-humoured smile, not the smile of the cynical. Perchance, we have been dreaming; dreaming a kind of nightmare. We suppose ourselves to be living in the year 1902. Motor-cars are rushing everywhere about. Telephones are

Points about Pedigrees

buzzing in our ears. An aerial ship is speeding through the air. Another ship is being navigated beneath the surface of the sea. An express train is seen in the distance, driven by electricity on a single rail, at the rate of sixty miles an hour. A pastoral people named Boers have forsaken their ploughs, and threaten to keep on fighting till the crack of doom. Some one touches us lightly on the shoulder, and we are wide awake, our own proper selves again. The whole surely is a dream! We are, in reality, citizens of London making preparations for the King's Coronation. Here are the King's crimson standards blazoned with gold, and here King Edward the Third's own chosen motto, " Dieu et mon droit," and here the ostrich plumes and the " Ich dien " of his son. Here, too,

The Coronation of Edward VII

are King Henry the Seventh's tall and portly Yeomen of the Guard, and here their captains, lieutenants, and exons. Garter King at Arms, in his magnificent tabard, is in his proper place, as are his historic supporters, Clarencieux and Norroy in theirs. Here, too, stand the six Heralds of old England —Chester, Lancaster, York, Somerset, Richmond, and Windsor, with their Pursuivants, Rouge Croix, Bluemantle, Rouge Dragon, and Portcullis. And here is his Grace the Hereditary Earl Marshal of England himself, Knight of the Most Noble Order of the Garter—Duke of Norfolk and Earl of Arundel. Save your Grace!

How strange in truth it all seems! Surely we may be forgiven the passing smile when we think of this present blending of the fourteenth and fifteenth with the twentieth century! Here are a number of, apparently, ordinary quiet-looking, ease-loving, home-keeping, middle-aged English gentlemen —distinguished enough in their respective stations, if you please, and as we for one most willingly admit ; here are these gentlemen ("great men all" by the roll), presently to be engaged in the acting parts of a most solemn and interesting ceremony, which takes us back eight hundred years to, at

Points about Pedigrees

least, the days of William the Norman, if not of his predecessor, Edward the Confessor. Where now are their armour, their helmets and gay-coloured plumes, their huge two-handed swords, fluttering pennons, and ponderous lances, their attendant esquires and pages, their gaily caparisoned armour-decked horses? Robes, ribbons, and coronets are all that now remain of these old-time paraphernalia. With a sight of them we must perforce remain content. For the rest, and as regards their  everyday life, most of these great lords, barons, bishops, viscounts, earls, marquises, dukes, the lord-archbishops of Canterbury and York, yea, even the Princes of the Blood Royal and his Most Gracious Majesty the very King himself ; all these great nobles, lords spiritual and temporal, and their

The Coronation of Edward VII

royal and imperial Master, in place of armour and helmet now array themselves in black silk hat and ordinary frock-coat! We are actually and indeed awake, and living in the twentieth century. The real and the shadowy alike provoke a smile. And, prithee, my right honourable friend, why not?

*   *   *   *   *

"The souls of emperors and cobblers are all cast in the same mould": so said the Seigneur de Montaigne, Lord of Montaigne (to give him his full title), sometime the pupil of George Buchanan, tutor of James the First of England, and a gentleman not unfamiliar in his time with princes and the humblest of their subjects too. Montaigne's dictum may be true enough; but even the soul of a cobbler may be cast in a finer mould than the majority of his fellows. In respect of his craft, truly, he may be able to trace his ancestry back to the very first cobbler who sat on the bench. It is conceivable that his progenitors of the remote past may have been persons of quality. Much more unlikely things have come to pass, than that a cobbler should be descended from a peer. One of the flock in most families, sooner or later, strays from the fold. His wanderings may lead him

Points about Pedigrees

to the top or the bottom, as his enterprise or energy, or lack of both may determine. Most of us, in our experience, have known of poor boys who, in the course of time, have attained to considerable wealth and distinction. "You say," once wrote a distinguished Professor of Oxford University to the compiler of these pages : "you say, in your article that my parents were poor, being farmers in a small way down in Devonshire. True ; but let me remark that I am exceedingly and justly proud of my parents and ancestry—poor, but of inestimable worth." Only the other day, I met a worthy man, of no sort of pretensions to refinement or even a grammar-school education, who had left his home in Yorkshire for America, a poor lad, with but very few shillings in pocket. He told me, that he had been compelled to borrow from another poor lad, his brother, to pay his passage across the ocean. Curiously enough he had followed his craft at the shoemaker's bench—may have been in very fact, for aught I know, a cobbler's apprentice in his native village. He is now the most considerable and by far the most wealthy manufacturer of boots and shoes in a well-known town in Massachusetts. His sons, both men of parts and education, are partners of their parent in the same prosperous business. Unless I am very greatly mistaken in these two gentlemen, they are proud to claim the relationship of sons with the one-time poor Yorkshire shoemaker, their father.

On the other hand, I was passing down Regent Street one day with a friend of mine who knows every one in London that it may happen I do not know. "Do you see that man?" said he, pointing to a "seedy," shambling, rickety-looking tramp. "Well, that man has paid me hundreds of pounds. He was one time one of the smartest officers of cavalry in the Queen's service." I never believed it possible that I could ever be brought to pass a person in London's streets, whom I had once claimed acquaintance with. I furtively did so on one occasion, when I recognised in a man standing at a street corner, intoxicated, filthy, ragged, squalid almost beyond recognition, one whom the world had once well known as a gentleman of exceptional professional attainments and of the first social standing. It is only when some are arrived at this condition—which Heaven, in mercy, guard each one of us against!—that neither interest nor pride is felt in tracing back ancestors, whether to cobblers or kings.

Points about Pedigrees

"Silent the Lord of the world
Eyes from the heavenly height,
Girt by His far-shining train,
Us who with banners unfurl'd
Fight life's many-chanc'd fight
Madly below in the plain.

"Hardly, hardly shall one
Come with countenance bright
*　　*　　*　　*　　*
Safe through the smoke of the fight,
Back to his Master again."

Truly, in respect of our industrious and esteemed friend, the cobbler: " I weigh the man, not his title ; 'tis not the king's stamp can make the metal better." " I have been inclined to think," wrote Addison in one of his more serious essays, " that there are greater men who lie concealed among their fellows, than those who come out, and draw upon themselves the eyes and admiration of mankind. . . . We are dazzled with the splendour of titles, the ostentation of learning, the noise of victories ; they on the contrary " (" they" here refers to those who may observe us from the spiritual world)—" they on the contrary see the philosopher in the cottage, who possesses his soul in patience and thankfulness, under pressure of what little minds call poverty and distress. They do

The Coronation of Edward VII

not look for great men at the head of armies, or
among the pomps of a court; but often find them
out in shades and solitudes, in the private walks
and by-paths of life. . . . The most famous among
us are often looked upon with pity, or with contempt,
or with indignation; while those who are most
obscure among their kind are often regarded with
love, with approbation, and esteem."

Now, in regard of the Imperial masters of mankind: "We owe a like obedience and subjection
unto all kings," wrote that prince of philosophers
already quoted, "for it respects their office; but
estimation and affection, we owe it only to their
virtue." Those only are truly great whose ambition
is to acquire the conscience of worthy enterprises,
rather than the prospect of worldly glory. "He
only is a great man who can neglect the applause
of the multitude, and enjoy himself independent of
its favour. This indeed, is an arduous task . . . it
is the highest step to which human nature can arrive.
Triumph, applause, acclamation are dear to the mind
of man; but it is a more exquisite delight to say to
yourself, you have done well, than to hear the whole
human race proclaim you glorious."

In conclusion I shall here add some extracts,

Points about Pedigrees

touching upon pedigrees, from the third part of that very curious and rare work, the "Boke of St. Albans" (1486), so scarce even in the days of Shakespeare, as to require to be set forth in a new form by Gervase Markham (1595), as "absolutely necessary and behoveful to the accomplishment of the Gentlemen of this flourishing ile, in the heroical and excellent study of armory." The extracts are from the original :—

"Insomuch thatt all gentilness (we read) commys of God of hevyn, at hevyn I will begin, where were V orderis of Aungelis, and now stand but IV, in cote armoris of knowledge encrowned ful hye with precious stones, where Lucifer with miliory's of Aungelis owt of hevyn fell unto hell and ordyr places, and ben holdyn ther in bonage, and all were erected in hevyn of Gentyll nature. A bondman or a churl wyll say all we be cummyn of Adam, so Lucifer with his cumpany may say all we be cummyn of hevyn."

Next follows how Gentilmen first began on earth, and how they are to be distinguished from Churles; or "Gentilmen from ungentilmen."

"Ther was never Gentilmen nor Churle ordeynyd by kunde, bothe had fadre and modre. Adam and

The Coronation of Edward VII

Eve had nother fadre and modre, and in the sonnys of Adam and Eve were founde bothe Gentilmen and Churle. By the sonnys of Adam and Eve, (Seth, Abell and Cayn,) devyded was the royall blode from the ungentill; a brother to sley his brother contrary to law, where might be more ungentilness? (What could be more ungentlemanly or vile? in Markham's edition.) By that dyd Cayn become a churle, and all his offspring after hym, by cursing of God and his own fadre Adam, and Seth was made a Gentilman thorow his fadre's and modre's blessing, and of the offspryng of Seth, Noe came a gentilman by kynde. Among Noah's 3 sons, Cham, Sem and Japhet, the two latter were Gentilmen, but Cham a proper Churle."

"Now to thee I give my curse wycked kaytiff for ever, and I give to thee the northe parte of the worlde to drawe thyne habitacion, for ther schall it be, where sorrow and care, cold and myschef as a Churle thow shalt have, in the third parte of the worlde wich schall be calde Europe, that is to say, the contre of Churlys.

"Japeth cum hyder my sonne, I made the a Gentilman to the weste part of the worlde, and to the occident end when as welth and grace shall be

Points about Pedigrees

so, then thyr habitacion shall be to take that other thirde parte of the worlde, wich schall be calde Asia that is to say, the contre of Gentilmen, and Sem my son, also a Gentilman, the oryente thow shalt take that other theirde parte of the worlde wich shall be called Affrica, that is to say, the contre of tempurnes.

"Of the offspring of the Gentilman Japheth come Habraham, Moises, Aron, and the profettys, and also the King of the right lyne of Mary, of whom that gentilman Jhesus was borne very God and man ; after his manhode kyng of the lorde of Jude Jues gentilmen, by is modre Mary prynce of cote armure."

We need procced no farther in these present disquisitions than to say, and that, too, without the need of appealing to mythological works, that few families are to be compared in antiquity with the Royal Family of England, of whom his Majesty King Edward the Seventh is the present Head and Representative. His Majesty's descent may be traced back to the Kings of England long prior to the Conquest. Through the grandmother of Henry II., wife of Henry I., he and his are the descendants of Alfred the Great, Egbert, and Cerdic, King of Wessex in the sixth century. Cerdic was believed to be a descendant of Woden, up to and even beyond

The Coronation of Edward VII

whom the genealogy is carried in the Anglo-Saxon Chronicle.

It is interesting to note that early royal titles—as Mr. Ashley states in " The Dictionary of English History "—were national, and not territorial. Thus, Egbert was " King of the West Saxons," and Alfred often used the title of " King of the Saxons." In view of Edward the Seventh's name, there is special interest in the style of Edward the Elder, who designated himself " King of the Anglo-Saxons." Athelstan was the first monarch to adopt regularly the title of " King of the English," which was also the official description of the Norman sovereigns. Magna Charta opens with the words, " John, by the grace of God, King of England, Lord of Ireland, Duke of Normandy and Aquitaine, and Earl of Anjou." Edward I. dropped the title derived from Normandy, but as compensation Edward III. added that of " King of France," which was retained till, strange as it may now seem, 1801. Another change was made in 1876, when Queen Victoria assumed the Imperial title of " Empress of India," and another change was made (of which more hereafter) in 1901.

PART I

The Accession, Proclamation, and Meeting of the First Parliament

OF

KING EDWARD THE SEVENTH

ACCESSION
OF EDWARD THE
SEVENTH

A T 6.30 p.m. on January 22nd, 1901, the greatly
beloved Queen Victoria died ; and on the day
following, her eldest son, Albert Edward, now King,
held his first Council at St. James's Palace, the
one interesting relic of the courts of Tudor, Stuart,
and Hanoverian sovereigns that London now owns.
Previously thereto the Lords of the Council, of
whom more than a hundred were present, the
Lord Mayor, Aldermen, and other officials of
the City of London, who attended in their robes
of office, and other noblemen and gentlemen,
who were also present, approved a Proclamation
announcing his Majesty as King Edward VII.
The Proclamation was signed by the members
of the Royal Family present, the Archbishops
of Canterbury and York, a large number of
other Privy Councillors, and by the Lord Mayor
and other representatives of the City of London.

35

The Coronation of Edward VII

Such was the official announcement as made in the *Court Circular* of the day.

The King attended the Council in semi-state, and Orders of Knighthood were worn by all entitled to do so. So far as the public were concerned, the first notice they received of the fact of the Council meeting was about twenty minutes to two, when the Sovereign's guard, consisting of an officer, a corporal-major, twelve gentlemen troopers, and a farrier of horse, trotted down the Mall of St. James's Park, and, turning along Marlborough yard, entered the grounds of Marlborough House. Meanwhile, the members of the Privy Council continued to arrive at St. James's Palace in large numbers, and there never was in the history of the English Court a gathering of the Privy Council so largely attended. It comprised, when assembled, no less than a hundred and eight members.

The City Fathers in traditional fashion attended, and were accompanied by the sword and mace bearers, the civic retinue, the Recorder, Town Clerk, City Solicitor, and other of the officials of the Corporation. They went in semi-state from the Mansion House by way of Queen Victoria Street, Embankment, Northumberland Avenue, and Pall

Accession of Edward VII

Mall, to the Palace. The cavalcade, which was escorted by a posse of mounted police, made a brave show, comprising about twenty carriages, the occupants wearing their robes and chains of office over levée dress so-called. Those attending, in addition to the officials mentioned, were (it might gratify some to preserve the record in this book) the Lord Mayor (Alderman Frank Green), Aldermen Sir Whittaker Ellis, Sir Henry Knight, Sir Reginald Hanson, Sir Joseph Savory, Sir David Evans, Sir Joseph Renals, Sir Walter Wilkin, Sir Horatio Davies, M.P., Sir Alfred Newton, Sir G. F. Faudel-Phillips, Sir Joseph Dimsdale, Sir Marcus Samuel, Messrs. Pound, Bell, Truscott, Alliston, Samuel Green, Strong, Smallman, Crosby, Sir John Knill, Sir W. P. Treloar, with the Sheriffs, Alderman Vaughan Morgan and Sir Joseph Lawrence.

It was about five minutes to two when the great gates of Marlborough House, opening on Pall Mall, were thrown open, and immediately the advanced point of the King's guard in full dress, the troopers bearing their carbines at the carry, emerged into the roadway. Then came the escort itself, with drawn swords, the feeble sun just adding a touch of glint to their polished helmets

The Coronation of Edward VII

and cuirasses. The officer of the escort rode beside the King's coach, which was driven at a trot. The King himself was in the uniform of a Field-Marshal, and wore his Orders and the blue riband of the Garter across his breast. He looked grave and somewhat worn, a circumstance that was, perhaps, not to be wondered at. By his side, in the uniform of the Norfolk Artillery Militia, was his Majesty's long-time friend, Lord Suffield, and he was also accompanied by Captain Holford, in the scarlet uniform of an equerry. There was an outburst of cheers as the King's coach was driven out of the grounds of Marlborough House, and, turning sharply into Marlborough Yard, it passed into the Mall, and thence into St. James's Palace by the Garden entrance. The throng in the Mall at this time was very great, and here again there was generous cheering, as if to assure the King that the people were with him in heart and sympathy.

By historic usage, said to date back several centuries, the Lord Mayor, Sheriffs, and Court of Aldermen of the City of London were informed that they might "give attendance" at the meeting of the Privy Council upon the accession of the

Accession of Edward VII

monarch "should they think proper." The letter
conveying such information was as follows:—

" PRIVY COUNCIL OFFICE,
"*January* 22nd, 1901

" Immediate.

"MY LORD,—The Lords of the Privy Council,
having been desired to meet at St. James's Palace
on Wednesday, the 23rd instant, at two o'clock p.m.,
I am directed to give your lordship notice thereof,
that your lordship and the Court of Aldermen may·
give attendance there if you should think proper.
Levée dress; crape on left arm.—I have the honour
to be your lordship's obedient servant,

"A. W. FITZ ROY.

" To the Right Hon. the Lord Mayor,
    " The Mansion House, London."

Needless to remark that the meeting of the
Privy Council was held in the interesting Banqueting
Hall of St. James's Palace, but the King did not
proceed there immediately. Ascending the main
staircase he passed into the Throne room—that in
which the Levées are held—and thence by Queen
Anne's room to the Picture gallery.

At the stroke of the appointed hour of two the
Duke of Devonshire, Lord President of the Council,

assumed the presidency of the assembly. The Duke made a formal communication of the death of Queen Victoria, and the succession to the Throne of her son, the Prince of Wales. It then became necessary to appoint a deputation to inform the King in the adjoining apartment that the Council had assembled. The Royal Dukes, with the Lord President, the Archbishop of Canterbury, and the Prime Minister were then directed to repair to the King's presence, and to acquaint him of the terms of the Lord President's statement. In a few minutes they returned accompanied by the King, who, we are told, was deeply moved.

His Majesty addressed the Council in what a member present on the occasion described as "a splendid speech, beautifully delivered," which occupied some seven or eight minutes. The King's address was finely dignified in tone, and at moments it seemed as if it were only with the greatest difficulty he was able to control his emotions. The title he would assume, he informed the Council, was Edward VII. There could only be, he said, one Albert, and that his revered father, Albert the Good. Then in earnest tones his Majesty pledged himself to devote his life to

Accession of Edward VII

the welfare of the country and the Empire, and in so doing he asserted his confidence in the support of Parliament and the people. The actual text of the King's speech, officially published in the *London Gazette*, was as follows:

"'Your Royal Highnesses, My Lords, and Gentlemen,—This is the most painful occasion on which I shall ever be called upon to address you.

"'My first and melancholy duty is to announce to you the death of My beloved Mother the Queen, and I know how deeply you, the whole Nation, and I think I may say the whole world, sympathise with Me in the irreparable loss we have all sustained.

"'I need hardly say that My constant endeavour will be always to walk in Her footsteps. In undertaking the heavy load which now devolves upon Me, I am fully determined to be a Constitutional Sovereign in the strictest sense of the word, and as long as there is breath in My body to work for the good and amelioration of My people.

"'I have resolved to be known by the name of Edward, which has been borne by six of My ancestors. In doing so I do not undervalue the name of Albert, which I inherit from My ever to be lamented, great and wise Father, who by universal consent is I think deservedly known by the name of Albert the Good, and I desire that his name should stand alone.

" 'In conclusion, I trust to Parliament and the Nation to support Me in the arduous duties which now devolve upon Me by inheritance, and to which I am determined to devote My whole strength during the remainder of My life.'

" Whereupon the Lords of the Council made it their humble request to his Majesty that his Majesty's Most Gracious Declaration to their Lordships might be made public, which his Majesty was pleased to Order accordingly."

The next proceeding was a solemn one—that in which the Lord Chancellor administered the oath to the King ; and immediately afterwards the Royal Dukes came forward, and, having taken the oath, each kissed the King's hand. They were followed by the Archbishop of Canterbury, and then the members of the Cabinet, who were sworn *en bloc*, each kissing the hand in succession. The Privy Council were also sworn as a whole, but the members did homage individually.

An unexpected difficulty (we have been told) arose in obtaining a copy of the King's speech in Council for publication in the special *London Gazette* above referred to. As a matter of fact, there was

The
Queen Consort's
Orb

The
Imperial
Orb

Temporal
Sceptre
(Victoria)

St. Edward's
Staff

Spiritual
Sceptre
(Victoria)

Accession of Edward VII

no copy, for the King had no notes and had not written his speech beforehand. As an extempore utterance it was, therefore, somewhat remarkable. Of course no shorthand writer was present to take notes, and the only way to obtain the copy was to ask his Majesty to dictate the speech to his secretary. His excellent memory enabled him to do this with accuracy.*

It may be interesting to add that the attendance of members of the Privy Council at this historic meeting included: The Duke of York, the Duke of Connaught, the Duke of Cambridge, Prince Christian, Field-Marshal Prince Edward of Saxe-Weimar, the Archbishop of Canterbury, the Prime Minister, the Earl of Clarendon, the Duke of Fife, the Lord Chancellor, the Speaker of the House of Commons, the Duke of Norfolk (Earl Marshal), the Duke of Rutland, the Duke of Northumberland, the Duke of Portland, the Earl of Coventry, Earl Carrington, the Earl of Chesterfield, Earl Spencer, the Earl of Kimberley, the Lord Chief Justice, Lord Rosebery, Lord Pirbright, Lord Rathmore, Lord Knutsford, Lord Morris, Lord Strathcona, Lord

* *Birmingham Post* (London correspondent), January 24th, 1901.

43

The Coronation of Edward VII

Rowton, Lord Brampton, Lord Balfour of Burleigh, Lord Goschen, Lord Lansdowne, Sir H. Campbell-Bannerman, M.P., Sir William Harcourt, M.P., Mr. J. Chamberlain, M.P., Sir S. Ponsonby Fane, Sir Richard Temple, Sir G. Goldie, Sir W. Hart-Dyke, M.P., Sir H. Drummond Wolff, Sir Francis Jeune, the Marquis of Hertford, Sir H. Fowler, M.P., the Chancellor of the Exchequer, Mr. John Morley, M.P., Mr. Asquith, M.P., Mr. Walter Long, M.P., Mr. J. W. Lowther, M.P., Mr. R. Spencer, M.P., Mr. Staveley Hill, Mr. Victor Cavendish, M.P., Mr. Arnold Morley, Mr. Lecky, M.P., Mr. Courtney, M.P., Mr. Bryce, M.P., Mr. Brodrick, M.P., Mr. Acland, Lord George Hamilton, Lord Ashbourne, Lord Burghclere, the Marquis of Ripon, Lord Cadogan, Lord Ribblesdale, the Earl of Cork, the Earl of Dartmouth, Lord A. Hill, Sir John Gorst, M.P., Mr. Jesse Collings, M.P., Lord Justice Romer, Lord Justice Smith, Lord Justice Charles, Lord Justice Rigby, Mr. W. L. Jackson, M.P., Sir John Kennaway, Mr. Seale Hayne, M.P., Mr. Akers-Douglas, M.P., the Lord Advocate, and Sir F. Milner. For the first time in the history of England the Proclamation of the Sovereign at the first meeting of the Privy Council was signed by Jews—

Accession of Edward VII

viz., Lord Pirbright, Sir George Faudel-Phillips, and Sir Marcus Samuel.

*   *   *   *   *

The aspect of the House of Lords soon after four o'clock of the afternoon of January 23rd, 1901, was unique. Instead of the regular set scene of a few members on the Ministerial side, and fewer on the Opposition benches, the way from the right of the Throne to the left of the Bar was thronged with Peers pressing forward to take the oath of allegiance to the Crown and the Constitution. All were in black, except the two Archbishops and the Bishops, whose white lawn sleeves and black satin robes gave the only relief to the throng of fully two hundred noblemen, old, young, and middle aged. At the Opposition side of the table stood a single clerk of the House of Lords in wig and gown to administer the oath and direct the signing of the roll. On the Woolsack sat the Lord Chancellor in black silk gown and full-bottomed wig. In the balcony on the Opposition side were about thirty ladies, all in deep mourning, giving to the assembly a greater air of solemnity than prevailed in the range of peers gradually moving along below.

The Coronation of Edward VII

The first of the Peers to take the oath and sub-scribe the roll after the Lord Chancellor were the Archbishop of Canterbury and the Archbishop of York. Each in turn shook hands with the Lord Chancellor, and passing a few members of the House of Commons, who were standing in front of the Throne, went out of the House. Other Peers followed, including the Duke of Connaught and the Prime Minister (Lord Salisbury).

Although it was announced officially that the House of Commons would not meet until four o'clock in the afternoon, a number of members came down early in the morning and secured seats. When the Speaker appeared, exactly at four o'clock, there were about two hundred members in their places. The Speaker took the chair and said :

"I would remind the House that by reason of the deeply lamented decease of her Majesty Queen Victoria, it has become our duty to take the oath of allegiance to her successor, his Majesty King Edward the Seventh. I will, according to ordinary custom, take the oath myself first, and then invite hon. members to come to the table and follow my example."

Accession of Edward VII

The Speaker then administered the Oath to himself as follows:

> "I, William Court Gully, do swear that I will be faithful and bear true allegiance to his Majesty King Edward the Seventh, his heirs, and successors, according to law. So help me God."

Having kissed the book, the roll was taken to the right hon. gentleman, and duly signed by him.

At ten minutes past six, 290 members having been sworn, the House adjourned until the next day at three o'clock.

The Parliamentary Papers for January 24th, 1901, cannot fail to be of interest to the student of history. The record of the previous day's sitting of the House of Lords ran thus:

> "House met, on the occasion of the Demise of her late Majesty Queen Victoria, pursuant to the Act of 6 Anne, c. 7. Prayers. The Lord Chancellor, singly, in the first place, took the Oath at the Table. Several Lords took the Oath. His Royal Highness the Duke of Connaught and Strathearn, singly, took the Oath. His Royal Highness the Duke of York, singly took the Oath."

The entry in the Journals of the House of Commons was as follows:

47

The Coronation of Edward VII

"It having pleased Almighty God to take to
his mercy our late Most Gracious Sovereign
Lady Queen Victoria of blessed memory, who departed this life yesterday between the hours of 6
and 7 of the clock in the evening, at Osborne House
in the Isle of Wight; and her late Majesty's Most
Honourable Privy Council, and others, having met
this day at Saint James's Palace, and having directed
that his Royal Highness Albert Edward Prince of
Wales be proclaimed King, by the Style and Title
of Edward the Seventh: Mr. Speaker, and several
other Members, came to the House of Commons
this day, where Mr. Speaker alone, and then the
other Members present, took the Oath, and several
Members made and subscribed the Affirmation
required by Law."

The title-page of the "Votes and Proceedings"
of the House of Commons was inscribed as relating
to "the Second Session of the 27th Parliament of
the United Kingdom of Great Britain and Ireland,
January 23rd, 1901, in the First year of the Reign
of his Majesty King Edward the Seventh."

PROCLAIMED KING
·· ʾAT Sᵀ JAMES' ··

ON Thursday, January 24th, 1901, the King was proclaimed at St. James's, and generally throughout London and the kingdom, with all the time-honoured ceremony. The cry "God save the King!" was then raised officially in the capital of England for the first time for over sixty years. It is of interest to recall that its earliest form was in every case associated with an Edward. Letters to Edward I. from one of his counsellors were accustomed to close with the formula, "Sire, Deu sauve e garde vostre noble seignurie e acresce vos honurs." The chronicler has it that the army of Edward III., when he landed in Flanders, in 1340, cried, "Vivat Rex Francorum et Angliæ"; and we get very near the present use in the poem "Edwardus Dei Gratia," written on the accession of Edward IV. :

> God save thy contenewannce
> And so to prospede to his plesaunce
> That ever thyne Astate thou mowte enhaunce!
> Edwardes Dai Gracia.

49

The Coronation of Edward VII

It was about the same period that another poem, highly complimentary to the English people, presented the precise phrase in the lines :

God, let neuere werre be vs among,
To lose that blo of gret renowne,
Ne neuere oure right be turned to wronge.
God save the Kyng, & kepe the crowne !

And the saying became consecrated to English use by the fact that, in the translation of the Bible made by Miles Coverdale, and a rendering followed by the Bishop's Bible and the Geneva Bible, and later by both the Authorised and Revised Versions, the phrase is more than once used. On the day above named, when Deputy Garter had read the Proclamation hereinafter set forth, as when Samuel proclaimed the first Hebrew monarch,

England's Tudor Queen.

50

Proclaimed King at St. James's

" all the people shouted and said, 'God save the King !'"

Forming three sides of a square, in the Friary Court of St. James's Palace, so inseparably interwoven with state ceremony from the days of the Tudors, a guard of honour of the Grenadier Guards was drawn up, with the King's Colour, and regimental band. Soon after eight o'clock a conspicuous figure on the balcony from which the proclamation was to be read was that of the Duke of Norfolk, who, in the capacity of Hereditary Earl Marshal of England, wore the scarlet tunic, gold-laced, of that time-honoured office, and the Riband of the Garter. A striking incident, which marked the near approach of the morning's ceremony, followed, in the arrival of the Headquarters Staff, brilliant in full-dress uniforms that imparted a welcome splash of colour to a scene so far sombre and grey. At the head of this cavalcade rode Earl Roberts, his breast gleaming with medals, and one hand holding his Field-Marshal's baton. Quickly recognised was the Commander-in-Chief, who wore his newly conferred Order of the Garter. He rode to a position immediately in front of the Generals of his Staff, among whom was Sir Evelyn Wood.

The Coronation of Edward VII

As the hour of nine rang out, it was to the quadrangle's red-draped balcony that all eyes were turned once more. For hither came the gorgeously arrayed officials who, with the Earl Marshal and Norroy King of Arms as central figures, bore so conspicuous a part in the day's ceremony. Accompanying the Deputy Garter were the historic personages of Heralds' College —to wit, York Herald, Somerset Herald, Windsor Herald, Rouge Croix Pursuivant, Bluemantle Pursuivant, and Rouge Dragon Pursuivant. All of these officials were arrayed in resplendent crimson tabards, upon which the Royal arms were embroidered in gold, and with them appeared the four Sergeants-at-Arms (their

THE HEADQUARTERS STAFF.

Proclaimed King at St. James's

collars worked in silver with S. S.) ; enormous gold maces, belonging to the Royal Insignia of the Tower, being carried by these attendants. To the front of the balcony there stept forward, when all was in readiness, the four State trumpeters, in brilliant uniform, and, ere Big Ben from the tower yonder, seen through the haze of the Park, had boomed the last of his nine strokes, an impressive fanfare of trumpets led up to the long-awaited Proclamation. Now, in clear, deliberate, ringing tones, so that not one word was lost to the hearing of those assembled in the courtyard, the Deputy Garter read from a long parchment scroll the Proclamation, as follows :—

" Whereas it has pleased Almighty God to call to His Mercy Our late Sovereign Lady Queen Victoria, of Blessed and Glorious Memory, by whose Decease the Imperial Crown of the United Kingdom of Great Britain and Ireland is solely and rightfully come to the High and Mighty Prince Albert Edward : We, therefore, the Lords Spiritual and Temporal of this Realm, being here assisted with these of her late Majesty's Privy Council, with Numbers of other Principal Gentlemen of Quality, with the Lord Mayor, Aldermen, and Citizens of London, do now hereby, with one Voice and Consent of Tongue and Heart, publish and proclaim, That the High and Mighty Prince, Albert

The Coronation of Edward VII

Edward, is now, by the Death of our late Sovereign of
Happy Memory, become our only lawful and rightful
Liege Lord Edward the Seventh, by the Grace of God,
King of the United Kingdom of Great Britain and
Ireland, Defender of the Faith, Emperor of India:
To whom we do acknowledge all Faith and constant
Obedience, with all hearty and humble Affection;
beseeching God, by whom Kings and Queens do reign,
to bless the Royal Prince Edward the Seventh, with
long and happy Years to reign over Us."

The final word of the Proclamation having been
spoken, Deputy Garter, in a voice that carried
beyond the old walls of the quadrangle to the ears
of the crowd standing without the Palace precincts,
cried out " God save the King ! " upon which the
State trumpets blared in unison once again, the
Grenadiers' band gave forth the National Anthem,
and a great burst of cheering went up from all
assembled. And so, with the inspiring words " God
save the King " still on the lips of his Majesty's
loyal subjects, the stately, picturesque, and impressive
rite in so far as St. James's was concerned reached
its appointed end.

A few minutes passed and then a procession
started on its way from the old Palace to different
points of the Empire's capital, where, in accordance

Proclaimed King at St. James's

with precedent, the Proclamation had to be read afresh. Mounted police led the way, and there was a brave escort of Royal Horse Guards (Blue). But the gorgeously clad Heralds and Pursuivants, departing in this instance from old-time custom, proceeded Citywards in closed equipages, and not, as seemed to be anticipated, on horseback. The General and officers of the Home District Staff brought up the rear of the cortége, which made its way along Pall Mall at a slow and stately pace to the ancient City ruled by the Lord Mayor. There in his presence all was done over again, and so elsewhere. At noon a Royal salute was fired in St. James's Park to mark the accession of King Edward VII. Thousands of people assembled on the Horse Guards' Parade to witness the ceremony.

ON Thursday, February 14th, King Edward VII. opened his first Parliament in person, accompanied by her Majesty Queen Alexandra, and attended by all the great officers of State. There, and then, from the Throne, in the House of Lords, the King made his "Solemn Declaration" --hereinafter referred to in Section VII. of the Coronation Service itself.

By the "Bill of Rights," 1688 (1 William and Mary, Sess. 2, c 2), it is enacted:

> "That every King and Queene of this Realme, who at any time hereafter shall come to, and succeede in, the imperiall crowne of this kingdome, shall on the first day of the meeting of the first Parlyament, next after his, or her, comeing to the crowne, sitting in his, or her, throne in the House of Peeres, in the presence of the lords, and commons, therein assembled, or at his, or her, coronation, before such person, or persons, who shall administer the coronation oath to him, or her, at the time of his, or her, takeing the said oath (which shall first happen), make, subscribe, and audibly repeate,

the Declaration mentioned in the statute made in
the thirtyeth yeare of the raigne of King Charles the
Second, entituled An Act for the more effectuall
Preserveing the King's Person, and Government, by
disabling Papists from sitting in either House of
Parlyament.

"But, if it shall happen that such King or
Queene upon his, or her, succession to the crowne
of this Realme, shall be under the age of twelve
yeares, then every such King or Queene shall make,
subscribe, and audibly repeate the said Declaration
at his, or her, coronation, or the first day of the
meeting of the first Parlyament as aforesaid, which
shall first happen after such King, or Queene, shall
have attained the said age of twelve years."

These words, "annexed to the original Act in a
separate schedule," are the law to-day in England—at all events to the date of this present
writing.

The Declaration above referred to (we append
it in the original) made by his Majesty was as
follows, the words being repeated after the Lord
Chancellor, the King kissing the Testament and
subscribing his name to the Oath immediately
after :—

"1 [Edward] doe solemnely and sincerely in the
presence of God professe testifie and declare, that I

doe believe that in the sacrament of the Lord's Supper there is not any transubstantiation of the elements of bread and wine into the body and blood of Christ, at or after the consecration thereof by any person whatsoever; and that the invocation or adoration of the Virgin Mary or any other saint, and the sacrifice of the masse as they are now used in the Church of Rome are superstitious and idolatrous, and I doe solemnely in the presence of God professe testifie and declare, that I doe make this declaration and every part thereof in the plaine and ordinary sence of the words read unto me, as they are commonly understood by English Protestants without any evasion, equivocation or mentall reservation whatsoever, and without any dispensation already granted me for this purpose by the Pope or any other authority or person whatsoever, or without any hope of any such dispensation from any person or authority whatsoever, or without thinking that I am or can be acquitted before God or man or absolved of this declaration or any part thereof, although the Pope or any other person or persons or power whatsoever should dispence with or annull the same, or declare that it was null and void from the beginning."

The Coronation Oath, it may be stated, is given in the Coronation Service, printed elsewhere : Section VII.

The scene in the House of Lords at the signing

Opens his First Parliament in Person

of the Declaration was thus graphically described in a London journal of the following day : *

"The chamber that we call the Royal Gallery is a worthy introduction to the House of Lords itself—the proportions admirable, the colour scheme sober and impressive. The two great battle-scenes of modern England—Waterloo and Trafalgar—line the walls in giant frescoes, pictures from which one's eye wanders to the touch of Georgian uniform in the head-dress and shakoes of some attendants of the Royal Household. The line is kept by the Yeomen of the Guard. Near the richly moulded doorway leading to the House itself stand the brilliant group of Gentlemen-at-Arms, their bedazzlement contrasting sharply with the pure white marble of the statue of the youthful Queen Victoria, idealised into a vision of loveliness and mild majesty. It is this statue that King and Queen face as they begin their progress up the Gallery.

"The staircase is a wonderful sight. On either side stands a living hedge of blue and silver topped with red plumes, and shining with the steel of swords and burnished cuirasses. It is the

* *Daily News*, February 15th, 1901.

The Coronation of Edward VII

Horse Guards. The officers group themselves at
the head of the stairway, and with them is a mass
of gayer plumage still—the Pursuivants and Heralds.
Gradually the forerunners and great figures of the
pageantry appear—Lord Salisbury rolling heavily
along in his scarlet peer's robes with three bars
of white ermine on the shoulder to mark his
rank. Apparently there is some doubt as to precedence, for he and the Duke of Devonshire, in
ducal dress, confer with very unceremonial smiles,
and presently the Prime Minister, whose position
here is Lord Privy Seal—for everything to-day is
ornamental rather than practical—takes his station
at the foot of the staircase. Then he returns,
and by-and-by from the Lords comes the Lord
Chancellor, with his long smoke-coloured wig and
white frilled necktie, and red and ermine robe with
touches of black in it. With him is the Mace,
and he, of course, is one of the great features of
the procession. By-and-by come the two officials
who are entrusted with the carrying of the twin
symbols of Sovereignty—the historic Crown of
England and the more mysterious Cap of Maintenance, with its broad ermine border and heavy
gold tassel. The Marquis of Winchester bears

The House of Lords from the River.

The Coronation of Edward VII

the Cap on a short stick, while the greater charge of the Crown is in the hands of the Duke of Devonshire [Lord President of the Council]. Round the Duke's neck is a band ; in front of him is a cushioned tray, on which lies the glittering symbol of majesty.

" It is impossible not to smile. The gravest of men, the Duke of Devonshire has the air of a State Autolycus, hawking some new ware of price. There is a long wait, then a stir at the closed doorway which leads from the Robing Room. Faint sounds of martial music are borne in from without, and then, suddenly, the small trumpeters, in their black jockey caps and long yellow coats, break into a flourish. The doors swing back, and the Royal procession marches in. Before it are marshalled the mingled pageantry of State and Court ceremonial, the Prime Minister, the Lord President, the Lord Chancellor, and the Household Officials. The Heralds link themselves on to the vanguard, and then, with little preface, come King and Queen, hand in hand, bowing slightly as they walk. Their dresses have a certain resemblance, a subtle union of masculine and feminine magnificence. The King wears a short

Opens his First Parliament in Person

ermine cape over his Field-Marshal's uniform, and beneath the cape a sweeping cloak and train of Royal purple. Some think his face recalls Harry Tudor ; we thought it rather Georgian. In the Queen's dress signs of mourning appear more distinctly and veil the strong contrasts of colour. On her head is a tiny, almost toylike crown of diamonds, and underneath it a sweeping black veil. Masculine eyes hardly grasp the subtle blending of black and purple in the long robe, and the Garter worn high up on the left arm. But the Queen's bearing is a thing to which no eye, however careless, can be indifferent. It is a touch of poetry, a feminine appeal which wins every heart. One thinks again of Queen Victoria's long-past youth and the girlish figure, the parted lips, the brave smile, of which all the courtly pens of sixty long years ago have told us.

* * * * *

"The procession is a little late, but here it is at last. The audience rises, and the brilliant group appears in the doorway. King and Queen are still hand in hand. They bow right and left, and the assembly bows lower still in silence. They

63

The Coronation of Edward VII

seat themselves, the Queen looking across the Peeresses' Gallery, the King gazing steadily before him. Then Black Rod breaks a long, rather awkward silence by slipping round to the Opposition side of the House, bowing low to the King as he goes. For it is still the fact that the presence of the Commons, of whom one hears so little in these high days, is needed before the Royal Message can be read, or the accompanying Declaration on the Mass can be made. And then occurs an amusing interlude. We are all attuned to a solemn mood, when on our listening ears breaks a noise as of thunder, a trampling of many feet, a shaking of the very galleries. It is the faithful Commons breaking in on our dignity—a Comus route of legislators. Somehow the dignified Speaker is in the centre, with Sir William Harcourt on his left and Mr. Balfour, Sir Michael Hicks-Beach, and presently Mr. Chamberlain, impelled from behind by some physical force or grace of courtesy, on the right. And then—the Commons having in some fashion assembled themselves before the bar —State reigns again.

"The prelude is a little out of tune with the later note of stateliness. The Lord Chancellor

Opens his First Parliament in Person

emerges from the group round the Throne, which now includes Lord Salisbury and the Duke of Devonshire (with the Crown) on the right of the Throne, and Lord Londonderry to the left, holding the Sword of State, with its elaborately worked hilt and scabbard. On chairs a little in front are a group of ladies in black—the daughters of the late Queen, the Duchess of Argyll among them, still notable for a certain stately beauty, the Duchess of Cornwall and young Prince Arthur of Connaught, while Prince and Princess Christian are somewhat in the background. It is to this group that Lord Halsbury presents himself armed with a red satchel of elaborate embroidery. His appearance proves to be the inauguration of the strange little ceremony, of which so much has been heard—the Declaration against the Mass and other Roman doctrines and observances. It is hardly impressive. King, and kneeling Chancellor, exchange copies of a Testament and of the Declaration form, from which the King proceeds to read out the rather crude, fierce sentences of the old formulary. Not a word, however, reaches ears—Catholic or Protestant—as distant as those in the Strangers' Gallery. The Chancellor follows [leads?] the King in a kind of rapid and muttered unison. Then comes the Oath, and the King's signature to the document, and again for a moment or two the ceremony proceeds on rather a halting wing. But it comes to a dignified and ample close. Now more at his ease, the Sovereign, who wears his cocked military hat, stands and reads the language of the King's Speech, which, as suiting the occasion, is far more rounded and ceremonial than usual. The effect is excellent. His strong, full voice penetrates easily every corner of the Chamber. The elocution is slow and dignified, and is altogether a lesson in the art of public speech to the statesmen who a few hours later replace him less audibly and less impressively. The Speech over, the King retains it folded in the hand which he gives to the Queen, and the pair make an exit not less stately than their entrance."

. One point arose out of the proceedings at the opening of the first Parliament of King Edward VII. which it may be interesting to note here. A protest, most temperately and respectfully worded, by the Roman Catholic peers against the form of the foregoing Declaration to which the King had to swear and subscribe was addressed to the Lord Chancellor (Lord Halsbury). That the oath was imperatively

Opens his First Parliament in Person

required by the statute which secures the succession to the Throne was not denied, nor did the signatories to the protest object to any forms which explicitly pledge the Sovereign to be true, in accordance with the " Bill of Rights," to the funda-

WESTMINSTER BRIDGE FROM THE SOUTH, SHOWING THE HOUSES OF PARLIAMENT.

mental principles of Protestantism. But they took exception to what they described as the contumelious epithets and the provocative tone of the oath, of which the text is printed, pp. 57-8. They expressed themselves as submitting to the law as it stood,

67

The Coronation of Edward VII

though they hoped it might be possible to alter it. They were, they said, as loyal and devoted to the Crown, and the King, as any others of his subjects. But the language of the Declaration to which the Sovereign had to subscribe on his Accession made it painful to them to be present on an occasion in which, from every other point of view, they shared the feelings of their countrymen. Those who read that Declaration can hardly be surprised in these days of religious toleration at this protest on the part of Roman Catholics whose loyalty would not be called in question.

The oath prescribed by the "Bill of Rights" was incorporated in the Act of Settlement, when the British people had just shaken themselves free from the tyranny of James II. and from the power of dispensation by the Pope, on which that Monarch relied in evading his Constitutional pledges. The circumstances have been altogether changed in the last two centuries. Similar oaths, as the *Times* * (from which we borrow these comments) points out —similar oaths by which private persons and ordinary officials were bound, have been modified so as to do away with offensive and contentious

* February 15th, 1901

matter. Yet there are still ample guarantees for the maintenance of the Protestant character of the British Constitution, which, indeed, will never be in any danger while the British people remain, as they will certainly remain, Protestant to the very marrow of their bones. An Act of Parliament bringing the language of the declaration to be subscribed by the Sovereign into harmony with the amenities of modern life might be passed, without touching any point of Constitutional policy, or giving the slightest opening for any conceivable advance of Roman Catholicism to political power by the exercise of personal influence over the ruling Sovereign.

Roman Catholics in both Houses of Parliament later complained of the Declaration, and recourse was had to a Joint Committee, to ascertain whether "the language of the Declaration could be modified advantageously, without diminishing its value for the continuance of the Protestant succession." This Committee recommended two changes—that the words referring to the adoration of the Virgin Mary should be struck out, and that a specific statement of belief in the Protestant religion should be inserted. When embodied in a Bill, however, the suggested alterations were exposed to severe criticism. Neither Roman Catholics nor English Churchmen were satisfied, and in the end the measure was abandoned, despite its second reading in the House of Lords (ninety-six for and six against) and the Prime Minister's (Lord Salisbury) avowal that unless the Declaration was modified as proposed it must remain in its old objectionable form.

*　　*　　*　　*　　*

Sterne writing to one of his friends remarks : " Of all the cants which are canted in this canting world —though the cant of hypocrisy may be the worst— the cant of criticism is the most tormenting." In truth, criticism is tormenting. The " Declaration " induced a great deal of it of one kind and another in speeches and writings; not a little of it, in Sterne's sense, "canting," and not a little of it, we willingly believe, sincere. His Eminence the Cardinal Archbishop of Westminster, had somewhat to say on the subject. In the view of his Eminence the " Declaration " as it stands is " blasphemous," " detestable," " an insult to Catholics," and "worthless as a guarantee for anything in the future."* Neverthe-

* Speech at Newcastle-on-Tyne, November 9th, 1901.

less, the Cardinal "entirely and frankly accepts the decision of the country that the King must . be Protestant." The "Declaration" doubtless is offensive in its phraseology to a good many ; but there it stands on the Statute book till Lords and Commons agree in abolishing or repealing it, and the People back them up in so doing. A modification of the "specially provocative" parts of the Declaration— that is to say, the "branding with contumelious epithets" of some of the doctrines held by the Roman Catholic subjects of the CROWN might with justice, perhaps, be conceded. But the mass of the nation would never be disposed, we believe, to go beyond that point.

M R. ADDINGTON, the well-known statesman of George III.'s reign, writing to his brother, remarks (December 29th, 1804) that he had just been dining with the King. "Our dinner consisted of mutton-chops and pudding." That frugal meal, served, be it observed, at Christmas-tide, and common to many a middle-class English household of to-day, whose wage-earning capacity hardly reaches to more than a couple of pounds a week, was served to Royalty and its guests at Buckingham House (then the Queen's palace), when its owner, King George III., was in receipt of £800,000 a year from the Civil List, plus other sources of income independent of Parliamentary control, which Mr. Burke estimated to amount annually to a sum "little less than a million pounds sterling."

A king may of course—just as one of his subjects —dine as he will, either in the style of Lucullus or Duke Humphry; and George III. was particularly partial (so we are told) to mutton, loin,

Will Serve for Table-Talk

leg, or shoulder. To provide a meagre dish of chops for a Minister of State (we think Chancellor of the Exchequer at that time) who had a voice in the voting of £800,000 a year "for the support of the dignity, and for the personal comfort of the Sovereign," was not, one would say, the wisest way of getting it increased when urgency demanded.

Yet George the Third found that sum insufficient, and was compelled more than once during his reign, to ask for more. Parliament voted substantial sums to pay his debts. His son, George the Fourth, annually received £845,727 for his Civil List—and a good deal more, amounting to at least three-quarters of a million pounds sterling, independent of Parliament. It is only fair to say, that the yearly charges on the Civil List were, in those days, exceptionally heavy for reasons various, all duly accounted for in the ample history of those times. Parliament eventually interfered to curtail those charges, and voted an annual sum to the Crown which may be said nowadays to represent the Sovereign's annual income from the State. William the Fourth received £510,000 a year, and her late Majesty Queen Victoria, £385,000, plus (if we remember aright) a matter of some £1200 a year, for what are now known as Civil List pensions, generally bestowed on the recommendation of the Prime Minister, on persons who have deserved well of the State in some profession, or department of public life, and whose means of livelihood are

BUCKINGHAM PALACE.

scanty. For example, Literature and Science, etc., share in these small annual benefactions; as occasionally do the widows and orphans of military and naval commanders.

I recollect a legal friend once telling me, that he had travelled to the country-seat of a very rich man to deliver some legal documents to be signed.

Will Serve for Table-Talk

My friend was invited to luncheon. Naturally, I asked the man of law—for all lawyers love good living—how he fared. Sumptuously, said he; delicious dishes and exquisite wines. The host himself partook of a single cup of cocoa, and a few pieces of dry toast. "'To such base uses may we come at last, Horatio,'" said I; "even though we be possessed of all the wealth of the Indies, and all the power of ancient Rome." 'Tis a melancholy reflection when we come to consider it, that imagination may "trace the noble dust of Alexander, till he find it stopping a bung-hole!" Though "not all the water in the rough wide sea, can wash the balm from an anointed king," not all that wealth e'er gave, or power conferred, can make him more than human. Parliaments may vote millions of money for the support of his dignity and for his personal comfort; but a king, after all, finds but twenty-four hours in a day, and can eat but his customary three daily meals, sleep his customary hours of sleep, enjoy himself occasionally as he will, walk, ride, rest, work, like the rest of us, during his three score years and ten or four score years of life, as may be allotted him.

Why do Parliaments haggle about "Civil Lists"

and Kings' incomes? What particular enjoyment
do kings get out of life more than the average of
us? I wonder whether Mr. Astor, Mr. Carnegie,
or Mr. Rockefeller—if they will forgive me for
naming them—or Mr. Any One Else could tell us
honestly that their enjoyment of life first to last
has been supreme—one continuous round of delight-
ful days all their life long? For my part, I would
vote his Majesty, a King, all the money he found
he had occasion for; trusting, perhaps, that none
but a very small amount would be required of him
who has but little to contribute. Such an expression
of opinion will be taken for what it is worth.
Literary persons rarely learn the value of money.
How should they? when so little comes their way.
But we are rambling from the point.

Many subjects which in old times were matters
of controversy with regard to the Civil List
of the Sovereigns of England have now disap-
peared. There is universal agreement that the
Civil List shall not contain anything but that
which is necessary for the maintenance of the
dignity and status of the Crown. In former reigns
frequent applications were made to Parliament, after
the Civil List had been fixed, for the payment

Will Serve for Table-Talk

of debts of the Sovereign or of members of the Royal Family. "Though in the later years of the late Queen's reign (Queen Victoria) the expenditure had been greater than Parliament had provided for, not one application," the Chancellor of the Exchequer told the House of Commons on the evening of March 11th, 1901, "had been made for any addition to the Civil List." "His Majesty King Edward," we were officially reminded, "had for many years occupied an exceptional position, having had, as Prince of Wales, the duties of Royalty thrown upon him, involving heavier expenditure than that ordinarily required of the Heir Apparent, yet his annuity fixed thirty years ago had proved sufficient for the exceptional duties which he had performed in a manner entitling him to the gratitude of the country, and to enable him to provide for all those who were dependent upon him in a spirit of generous consideration for their comfort and welfare which had been an example to the nation at large."

Both these statements, it may be remarked in passing, came as a surprise to those who, in time past, were seldom free from gossiping about the late Queen's supposed thrift on the one hand,

The Coronation of Edward VII

and the Prince of Wales's supposed extravagance on the other : another lesson on the un-
righteousness and injustice of judging others. " The
basis of the proposals of the Government were
the Civil List of her late Majesty, with such varia-
tions as the altered circumstances and experiences
of more than sixty years might show to be necessary.
There never was a time when the Monarchy was
more universally popular, and it was incumbent
upon the people as a matter of honour to provide
adequately for the dignity of the head of the State.
At the same time, all would agree that that should
be done without extravagance or lavish waste."
Such were the views of his Majesty's Government,
in making arrangements for the due support of
the King's dignity, and in furtherance of the
comfort of his Majesty's Household and that of
Queen Alexandra, and the members of their
family when Parliament took the Civil List into
consideration last year.

On April 4th, 1901, the House of Commons Committee, to which the whole matter had been referred,
published its report, and all the facts and suggestions
therewith associated. The financial recommenda-
tions of the Committee may be thus summarised :

Will Serve for Table-Talk

1. Civil List			£470,000
First Class .	Their Majesties' Privy Purse . . .	£110,000	
Second Class .	Salaries of his Majesty's Household and Retired Allowances . .	125,800	
Third Class .	Expenses of his Majesty's Household	193,000	
Fourth Class .	Works . . .	20,000	
Fifth Class .	Royal Bounty, Alms, and Special Services . . .	13,200	
Sixth Class .	Unappropriated .	8,000	
	Total for the Civil List . .	£470,000	
2. Annuity to H.R.H. the Duke of Cornwall and York (later created Prince of Wales) . .			20,000
3. Annuity to H.R.H. the Duchess of Cornwall and York (Princess of Wales)			10,000
4. Provision for the King's Daughters . . .			18,000
5. Charge on Consolidated Fund for Household Pensions to Servants of the late Queen, not exceeding			25,000
	Total		£543,000

On Thursday, May 14th, 1901, the Chancellor of the Exchequer (Sir Michael Hicks Beach) brought the proposals of the Government, in respect of the Civil List—the King's annual income, to use an everyday term—before the House of Commons.

79

The Coronation of Edward VII

The following resolution was put from the Chair:—
" That there shall be charged on the Consolidated
Fund, as from the demise of her late Majesty, the
following annual payments:—For the King's Civil
List, £470,000; for retired allowances, such sums
as may be required for the payment in each
year of pensions granted by her late Majesty or
by his present Majesty to servants of her late
Majesty's household, not exceeding £25,000; for
Civil List pensions, such sums as may be required,
taken in each year, for Civil List pensions,
already granted or hereafter to be granted; for
the Duke of Cornwall and York, £20,000; for
the Duchess of Cornwall and York, £10,000;
for the Duchess of Cornwall and York, in the
event of her Royal Highness's surviving the Duke
of Cornwall and York, £30,000; for his Majesty's
daughters, £18,000; for Queen Alexandra, in the
event of her Majesty's surviving his Majesty the
King, £70,000; and that provision be made for
continuing for a period of six months after the
close of the present reign certain items charged,
which would otherwise be then determined." It
was carried by a majority of 249 in a " House"
of 365 members. The Duke of Cornwall and York,

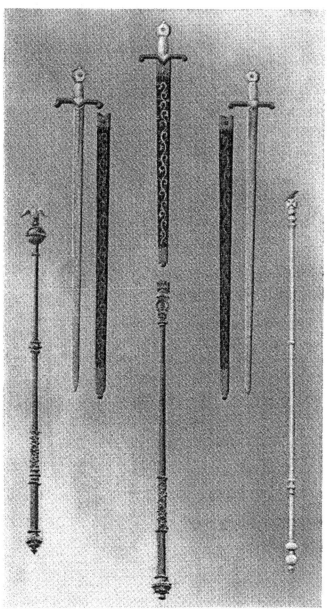

Spiritual
Sceptre
(William IV)

Sword
of
Mercy
(Sheathed)

Ivory Sceptre
(Anne Boleyn)

Temporal
Sword of
Justice

Temporal
Sceptre
(William IV)

Sword of
Spiritual
Justice

Will Serve for Table-Talk

it should be noted, was created Prince of Wales on November 9th following.

With the resolution no serious fault was found in any quarter. It was generally conceded that, without being lavish, the provision made for the Crown was sufficient to secure in the actual circumstances of the time the maintenance of its honour, dignity, and necessary ceremonial.

Referring to the debate that took place on this proposal the *Times* * said : " Comparing the present occasion with the last upon which the Civil List came before Parliament for revision, it is impossible to miss the significant alteration in the temper of the House and the country. There is not a trace of the somewhat grudging spirit which then prevailed. At a time when the national burdens are exceptionally heavy, a substantial addition to the cost of the Monarchy meets with nothing but general approval. It is quite true that in relation to the general expenditure of the country the increase of the Civil List is a mere trifle. But it is equally true that it is quite large enough to have provoked serious opposition in a different condition of public sentiment.

* May 15th, 1901.

The Coronation of Edward VII

"What is the cause of the marked change in the mode of looking at the Civil List? There can be no sort of doubt that it is due to the cause assigned by Sir Michael Hicks Beach, the great popularity which has accrued to the Crown owing to the admirable manner in which Queen Victoria discharged all the duties of a constitutional Sovereign. At her accession the country had had Sovereigns of a very different type to contemplate for several generations. The Crown was not popular, certainly no one would have ventured to say of it that 'at present it is, perhaps, the most popular of our great institutions' as Sir Michael Hicks Beach said last night, without calling forth a murmur of dissent. While rendering all homage to the late Queen for the great qualities and the consistent devotion to duty which endeared her to her people and strengthened the foundations of the Throne, we may add that something more was required to produce the condition of public feeling and temper upon which we may now congratulate ourselves. Respect for his mother would not by itself have produced the existing unanimity, in providing upon an increased scale for the expenditure of the King. If Queen Victoria differed widely from the Georges, so did her Heir Apparent differ

82

Will Serve for Table-Talk

widely from the type of Heir Apparents to which the country had been accustomed. Instead of being a leader of faction and a centre of intrigue, he was the most loyal and one of the most hard-working of her Majesty's subjects. He bore himself in his difficult position with a tact, a wisdom, and a dignity which the nation fully appreciated. At his accession to the Throne he was hailed with enthusiasm and an assured confidence which count for much, even beside the memory of the virtues which adorned the late Queen."

PART II
THE CORONATION

HE·THAT·WEARS·THE CROWN·IMMORTALLY LONG·GUARD·IT·YOURS

"The perfection of Glory consists in these three particulars: That the People love us; that they have confidence in us; that being affected with a certain admiration towards us, they think we deserve honour."

"THE sharpest and most difficult profession of the world, in mine opinion" (wrote old Montaigne, in the middle years of the sixteenth century), "is to act and play the King. I excuse more of their faults, than commonly other men do ; and that in consideration of the down-bearing weight of their charge." "The person who is the cause of all this pomp and magnificence is the man I envy least," Prince Charles Edward is reported to have remarked (on the authority of David Hume *) to a gentleman who recognised him in the Abbey at the Coronation of George III. On the other hand, when, at the coronation of Queen Mary (wife of William the Third), the Princess Anne kindly remarked to the Queen: "Madame, I pity your fatigue," "A crown, sister," said her Majesty—"sharply," so Oldmixon would have us believe—"is not so heavy as it seems."

* *The Gentleman's Magazine*, 1773.

The Coronation of Edward VII

We are inclined to think that, in these our own times, "the down-bearing weight" of the King's charge, not less maybe than his crown, is not so heavy, perhaps, as might without consideration appear to be. Truly, his Majesty's charge is sufficiently onerous in all conscience—in the ordinary daily duties to be performed, in the time and personal attention necessary to be given to those duties, in ceremonial functions to be presided at— Drawing-rooms, Levées, and the like, in Council meetings and interviews with Ministers of State, in a hundred-and-one fatiguing other affairs, which the King's subjects pray his Majesty from time to time to take part in, wholly unconnected with his more serious and imperative duties as Sovereign. What those daily duties were, and how exacting they were, in the late Queen Victoria's reign, we were told by the Queen herself in her letters to

"The King shall have Welcome"

her People. Day in and day out, they had to be undertaken by the Queen, much as the daily routine of one of the least important officials of the State. When one comes to consider of it, very few would be willing to exchange the leisure of a subject for the labour of a King.

The amount of business a King disposes of in the course of a working day must be out of all proportion greater than the average entailed upon very many of his subjects. From the standpoint of merely personal convenience, there is probably no measure to which his Majesty of England would more thankfully say " Le Roy le veult "—after the manner of the Royal assent in old Norman French given to measures passed by Parliament—than one for restricting the labours of all Britons, including himself, to eight hours a day. Such at least is the opinion of a contemporary London journal.* To the multifarious and most responsible duties devolving upon the Sovereign, have been super-added in his Majesty's case a thousand and one cares arising out of his accession to the Throne. Few people have any idea of the time and thought required for the arrangement of such a great Court

* *The Daily Telegraph*, November 9th, 1901.

The Coronation of Edward VII

function as the Coronation. When all the machinery
of an historic public ceremony is finally set in
motion, it works so smoothly that those who only
watch its frictionless movement fail to realise that
this very ease is the outcome of months of patient
consideration and forethought. But the busiest
man has always the most leisure at his disposal,

THE KING'S GUARD AT ST. JAMES'S PALACE.

and the King has never allowed these supplemen-
tary taxes upon his time to interfere with the first
pledge he gave to the nation to devote his life,
as his ever-to-be-lamented mother did before him,
to the interests and welfare of the Empire over
which he rules. Ministers alone could give a detailed account of the care and attention which his

"The King shall have Welcome"

Majesty bestows on concerns of State, and their lips are sealed. But the general public has formed an adequate idea of the intense devotion of Queen Victoria to public affairs, and it is in her footsteps that King Edward is travelling.

The model of a Constitutional Sovereign! How often we have heard that phrase? Englishmen never fail to point with pride to the fact, that her late Majesty Queen Victoria was that very model, illustrious in character and in example alike. The fact that it is so and was so, does not appear to have lessened the good Queen's labours one jot. On the contrary, it probably largely added to them, since among the chief obligations entailed upon a constitutional sovereign is that paramount sense of duty that impels him always vigorously and religiously to fulfil his own. "Every subject's duty is the King's." How awfully difficult it is for the greatest or meanest among us, the most eager, the most earnest, the most prudent, the most unselfish, to come anywhere near a rigorous and religious fulfilment of ours!

"The appearance of power," wrote Lord North, "is all that a King of this country can have." We should imagine—with every feeling of respect be it added—that a King of England should be very well content to find he has no more. For the King's trusted Ministers to do all the thinking and working, and the King himself to have all "the appearance of power," and (as Lord North added) "to be treated with all sort of respect and attention" would, one might suppose, be one of the happiest conditions in which a King could find himself placed. Is it going too far to express the hope that, under such conditions, King Edward the Seventh will be crowned in the ancient coronation chair of our kings at Westminster? None of its former occupants ever had more abundant assurance than he that the "down-bearing weight" of the King's charge will be cheerfully lessened by the affectionate respect and loyalty of his subjects.

Not less fortunately for a King of England, than for his subjects: "There can be no exercise of prerogative," so said Sir Samuel Romilly on a memorable occasion, "in which the King is without some adviser. He might seek the counsels of any man however objectionable, but that man would be responsible for the advice given, and for the acts of the Crown. There was no Constitutional doctrine more important than this, for the protection of the Crown. History had unfolded the evils of a contrary principle having prevailed." Lord Erskine also on a like occasion, in the House of Lords, declared: " The King can perform no act of government himself; and no man ought to be received within the walls of this House to declare that any act of government has proceeded from the private will, and determination or conscience of the King. The King as chief magistrate can have no conscience which is not in the trust of responsible subjects. When he delivers the seals of office to the officers of State, his conscience, as it regards the State, accompanies them. . . . No act of state or government can therefore be the King's. He cannot act but by advice; and he who holds office sanctions what is done, from whatever source it may proceed."

According to Lord Macaulay: " The doctrine that the Sovereign of the United Kingdom is not responsible, is doubtless as old as any part of our English constitution. The doctrine that his Ministers are responsible is also of immemorial antiquity. That where there is no responsibility, there can be no trustworthy security against maladministration is a doctrine which, in our age, and country, few people will be inclined to dispute. From these three propositions it plainly follows, that the administration is likely to be best conducted, when the Sovereign performs no public act without the concurrence and instrumentality of a Minister. This argument is perfectly sound. But we must remember that arguments are constructed in one way, and governments in another. In logic, none but an idiot admits the premises and denies the legitimate conclusion. But, in practice, we see that great and enlightened communities often persist, generation after generation, in asserting principles, and refusing to act upon those principles. It may be doubted whether any real polity that ever existed has exactly corresponded to the pure idea of that polity. According to the pure idea of Constitutional Royalty, the prince reigns and does not govern ; and Constitutional Royalty as it now exists in England comes nearer than in any other country to the pure idea. Yet it would be a great error to suppose (the Historian adds) that our princes reign and never govern." However that may be : " Ours is the happiest, the best, the most noble Constitution in the world ; and I do not believe it possible to make a better." If any should be disposed in

"The King shall have Welcome"

these days to disagree in that opinion, perhaps they might find some degree of justification for a discussion upon the point, in the fact that the words were spoken by Lord Bradfield, Lord Justice Clerk of Scotland's High Court of Justiciary in Edinburgh, in the year 1793, at the trial of Thomas Muir for sedition. Even Judge Jeffreys has found his latter-day apologists. Perchance Bradfield may find his—not for the words now quoted, but for some of his acts as judge.

Mr. Gladstone, in one of his constitutional essays, dwells with characteristic fervour upon the immeasurable gulf between the Crown and the most highly placed of subjects. Philosophers, conscious or unconscious, may ask with Uncle Toby, 'What is all that to a man who fears God?' But from the conventional and constitutional point of view, Mr. Gladstone was perfectly right. The British Constitution has been studiously framed to exalt the person of the Sovereign above all possible rivalry and amenability to any human tribunal. When the French King was naughty in the schoolroom another boy was whipped. For the acts or omissions of a British Sovereign a British

The Coronation of Edward VII

Minister is always responsible. The Sovereign is approached with profound reverence, he is carefully shielded from profane observation (this care is, so it seems to us, less seriously attended to than formerly), and his name cannot be so much as mentioned, except as a pure form, in Parliamentary debate. Mr. Disraeli was severely and justly blamed because, after his defeat on the Irish Church Resolutions in 1868, he intimated to the House of Commons that the Queen had expressed a preference for one of two possible courses. That is precisely the sort of thing which a Minister has no right to say. The Crown is an impalpable, intangible entity, which its confidential servants are bound to shield and to protect. The individual Sovereign may by personal influence, and still more by personal example, exercise an immense power for evil or for good. The King had in one respect a great advantage, while from another point of view he laboured under a serious difficulty. He succeeded a very great and a very good woman, 'the pillar of a people's hope, the centre of a world's desire.' He can hardly hope to surpass her. But if he follow in her footsteps, he cannot go far wrong.

" The King shall have Welcome "

" The King when he came to the throne was the oldest Heir Apparent in Europe. He was also the best known. It is accounted among not the least of the services which he has rendered to his country, that he cultivated with perfect success the Royal families of Europe, and the Republic of France. In Paris he was always welcome. He showed that he liked the French, and they welcomed him with cordial enthusiasm. An excellent linguist, a genial companion, and a cosmopolitan man of the world, he took away, so far as he could, the reproach of insular coldness and pride which is attached with more or less justice to the British nation. He made himself at home in France; and in Germany he was at home by nature. With the House of Romanoff he is doubly connected, and he was on peculiarly intimate terms with the father of the present Czar, as he is with the Czar himself.

" At home the King always set in public an admirable example of what an Heir Apparent should be, and fulfilled with entire success the singularly arduous task of being actively neutral in politics. Interested, and well known to have been interested, in all that was going on, King Edward when Heir Apparent never, with one exception,

showed the faintest preference for one side of a
political controversy against another. That exception was the Deceased Wife's Sister Bill, for
which he always steadily voted. As Prince of
Wales he was equally courteous, agreeable, and
attentive to all leading politicians without regard
for their principles or their votes. The public
did not know whether the King as Prince of Wales
was Liberal or Conservative, Home Ruler or
Unionist, Jingo or Pro-Boer. With all his mother's
Prime Ministers he was on cordial terms. From
the personal prejudice against Mr. Gladstone
which is said to have prevailed in the circles of
the Court, he was conspicuously free. His gracious
and sympathetic kindness to Mrs. Gladstone at the
funeral of her illustrious husband was observed by
every one present. With Lord Beaconsfield and
Lord Salisbury he was on the best of terms.

"Lord Rosebery, the only other Prime Minister he
can have really known, is known to be one of
his most intimate friends. There can, indeed, be
no higher testimony of his fitness for the splendid
position which he fills as King than the fact that
as Prince of Wales all parties respected him,
while no party could claim him for its own.

"The King shall have Welcome"

Practical politicians only can realise how much self-control and self-suppression this means. For the Prince, like other Englishmen, must have had opinions. It was his high resolve, which he kept, that he would act as if he had them not." We take leave to borrow these excellent and entirely true opinions from a leading article in the *Daily News* of January 24th, 1901, while it was yet under the editorship of one of the ablest of English journalists, and represented in its columns generally the best traditions of the Liberal Party in English politics.

*   *   *   *   *

Nihil est tam populare quam bonitas. Nothing is so popular as goodness is, "and never was there time, or place, wherein more assured and great reward was proposed unto Princes, for goodness and justice. . . . Let him shine over others with humanity, with truth, loyalty, temperance, and above all with justice. . . . It is only the People's will wherewith he may effect what he pleaseth; and no other qualities can allure their will so much as they, as being the profitablest for the people." So wrote Montaigne, before quoted, at a time when such virtues in princes were rare—"markes

The Coronation of Edward VII

nowadays rare, unknown, and exiled among kings" as he quaintly observes. "Such markes,"—albeit four centuries of history have wrought vast changes in the characteristics of kings, no less than in their kingdoms and people : "such markes," may it not be said, 'are of equal value and import now, as in time past ; for, truly, nothing is so popular as goodness is, whether in respect of kings or their subjects.

It was this quality, exhibited in such abundant measure, in the character of Queen Victoria, that made her so greatly beloved by her subjects, and of so great fame the world throughout. Her son, our present King, has shown a disposition to "allure" the people's will by the cultivation of the same quality. It has been truly said of him that he is of an expansive and genial disposition, and extremely popular with all classes of his subjects. As leader of society, King Edward is admirably equipped. He is celebrated all over Europe for his perfect manner, his genial and gracious address, and his remarkable faculty for saying exactly the right thing at the right moment. His Majesty has warm personal friends in every European Court, and near relatives in, one might almost say, each of them. He has a wide experience of men and

"The King shall have Welcome"

affairs, and understands that display and the panoply of State are absolutely necessary to the dignity and prosperity of the nation, superficial as in a sense they are. It is certain that the King, if not himself partial to State display, has recognised its importance in the social life of England, and especially that of London, where in the Season, so-called, anything of that nature attracts strangers, and in various degrees contributes to the advantage of trade, and in no small measure to that section of trade which, at the West End of London, trusts so largely to the influence and support of a resident Court and wealthy aristocracy. For many years of the late Queen's life London was without a resident Court. It is likely that King Edward will stay much more frequently at Buckingham Palace, than was the case with Queen Victoria, after the death of the Prince Consort.

Had it not been for King Edward and Queen Alexandra when Prince and Princess of Wales, London would have been practically without any Season at all. No man in public life worked harder than the Prince to keep things moving. He was constantly presiding at banquets, and at public meetings, and doing his utmost to promote

The Coronation of Edward VII

the success of the Season, often perilously threatened
(for reasons we admit as sufficient) by the absence
of the Court and its *entourage.* Condemned day
after day to gigantic luncheons, monster dinners,
and interminable festivities of one kind and another,
he seldom hesitated to sacrifice his own personal
ease and comfort to his sense of public duty. The
Prince's labours year after year were interminable,
in so far as state and social functions and festivities
were concerned. His inaugurations of public buildings and exhibitions, unveiling of statues, laying
of foundation stones, the speeches he never failed
to make on such occasions, and the speeches and
addresses he had to listen to, the multitudinous
meetings he was ever ready to preside at : if these·
things were related in full, among the other duties
of his Majesty, fulfilled when he was Prince of
Wales, the catalogue of these alone would fill a
volume.

King Edward acquired universal popularity by
his willing attention to such duties ; duties
incumbent upon a Prince, whose desire is to gain
and keep the loyalty and affection of those one
day to become his subjects. Irksome as such
matters of daily duty must often have been to

" The King shall have Welcome "

himself, they are nevertheless important in many ways in the social and political life of the nation.

* * * * *

" The future King of England," now his present Majesty Edward the Seventh, to whom God grant long Life and Happiness, and the full and free loyalty and goodwill of his subjects ; " the People's will wherewith he may effect what he pleaseth " : " the future King of England (I read in a book published some fifteen years ago)* is chiefly distinguished from many of his countrymen by his complete freedom from arrogance. His courtesy is exquisite, his grace of manner irresistible. He throws himself entirely into the matter that for the moment engages his attention, and makes each favoured person to whom he speaks believe that he is an object of special consideration. His friends say, that with them he forgets his rank ; but it is only on condition that they remember it ; and his familiarity with others is not theirs with him." But, these are twice-told tales, scarce worth the relating now, save in so far as they serve to illustrate the personal qualities of his Majesty. Surely England never had a more popular Prince,

* " The World of London," Count Paul Vasili.

than he who for so many years signed himself "Albert Edward, Prince of Wales," now about to be crowned King in Westminster Abbey. He is King already "to effect what he pleaseth," by his people's will, having so stoutly and fairly striven to gain their goodwill in preceding years, when Prince of Wales.

*　　*　　*　　*　　*

As this book seeks to record every important event in the first year of King Edward the Seventh's reign, pertaining to his Majesty's circumstances as Ruler of the Empire, it will be convenient to state here that his first Parliament passed a measure authorising certain changes in the Royal title.

It was very generally felt that the creation and inauguration in 1901 of the Australian Commonwealth, together with the overwhelming proofs of loyalty to the Empire afforded by the Colonies during the South African war, ought to be recognised by some change in the Royal style. Accordingly both Houses of Parliament gave their ungrudging support to a Bill enabling the King to accomplish the purpose in view by means of a proclamation. Such proclamation was made November 4th, 1901, as follows :—

" The King shall have Welcome "

" EDWARD, R.I.

" WHEREAS an Act was passed in the last Session of Parliament, intituled ' An Act to enable His Most Gracious Majesty to make an Addition to the Royal Style and Titles in recognition of His Majesty's Dominions beyond the Seas,' which Act enacts that it shall be lawful for Us, with a view to such recognition as aforesaid of Our Dominions beyond the seas, by Our Royal Proclamation under the Great Seal of the United Kingdom issued within six months after the passing of the said Act, to make such addition to the Style and Titles at present appertaining to the Imperial Crown of the United Kingdom and its Dependencies as to Us may seem fit : And whereas Our present Style and Titles are, in the Latin tongue, ' Edwardus VII. Dei Gratiâ Britanniarum Rex, Fidei Defensor, Indiæ Imperator,' and in the English tongue, ' Edward VII., by the Grace of God of the United Kingdom of Great ·Britain and Ireland King, Defender of the Faith, Emperor of India,' We have thought fit, by and with the advice of Our Privy Council, to appoint and declare, and We do hereby, by and with the said advice, appoint and declare that henceforth, so far as conveniently may be, on all occasions and in all instruments wherein Our Style and Titles are used, the following addition shall be made to the Style and Titles at present appertaining to the Imperial Crown of the United Kingdom and its Dependencies ; that is to say, in the Latin tongue, after the word ' Britanniarum,' these words, 'et terrarum transmarinarum quœ in ditione sunt Britannicâ'; and in the English tongue, after the words 'of the United Kingdom of Great Britain and Ireland,' these words, 'and of the British Dominions beyond the Seas.'"

Those versed in historical and antiquarian lore will recall the fact that, in the course of centuries, the sovereigns of England have frequently changed their styles. William I. (for example), surnamed the Conqueror, who was but duke in his own Normandy, contented himself with the description "Rex Anglorum," but he is alone in his simplicity, possibly because he never felt too secure of remaining King of England. William II. was "Dei gratiâ, rex Anglorum"; Henry II. was "Rex Angliae, dux Normaniae et Aquitaniae"; John, the first to make reference to the sister island, was "Rex Angliae et dominus Hiberniae"; Henry III. added "dux Aquitaniae"; Henry V. was "Rex Angliae, haeres et regens Franciae et dominus Hiberniae"; Henry VI. was "Dei gratiâ, rex Angliae et Franciae et dominus Hiberniae"; Henry VIII. was "Dei gratiâ, Angliae, Franciae et Hiberniae rex, Fidei Defensor, et in terrâ Ecclesiae Anglicanae et Hibernicae Supremum Caput."

"The King shall have Welcome"

The climax of length was reached when Mary came to the throne. She and her Consort were "By the Grace of God, King and Queen of England and France, Naples, Jerusalem, and Ireland, Defenders of the Faith, Princes of Spain and Sicily, Archdukes of Austria, Dukes of Milan, Burgundy, and Brabant." Elizabeth was merely "Queen of England, France, and Ireland, Defender of the Faith." James I. was "King of England, Scotland, France, and Ireland, Defender of the Faith." William and Mary were the same, but in the plural number. Queen Anne, after the Union with Scotland, was "Queen of Great Britain, France, and Ireland." George I. was "King of Great Britain, France, and Ireland, Duke of Brunswick-Luneburg, Defender of the

QUEEN ELIZABETH IN HER ROBES OF THE ORDER OF THE GARTER.

107

The Coronation of Edward VII

Faith." George III. on January 1st, 1801, discarded the French title (as well he might) and became, by Royal proclamation, "Dei gratiâ, Britanniarum rex, fidei defensor"; and her late Majesty was "By the Grace of God, of the United Kingdom of Great Britain and Ireland, Queen, Defender of the Faith, Empress of India." "Empress of India" came in the latter days of Lord Beaconsfield's administration of affairs. Queen Victoria was so proclaimed at Delhi, January 1st, 1877.

* * * * *

The King's Tudor Title "Defender of the Faith" was not permitted to pass unchallenged, in the various newspaper discussions that arose out of the "Declaration," elsewhere referred to. But, as was pertinently pointed out, the King, in the Coronation ceremony, receives a ring from the officiating Archbishop "as an emblem of kingly dignity and of defence of the Catholic Faith." The Church of England, which the Sovereign is solemnly pledged to maintain and defend, officially and explicitly teaches that "before all things it is necessary to hold the Catholic Faith." The Catholic Faith, defined in the three common creeds of Catholic Christendom—the Apostles' Creed,

"The King shall have Welcome"

namely, the Athanasian and the Nicene, each professed by Protestants of the Church of England —is necessarily the same now as when those creeds were promulgated. It is this Faith of which the King is styled "Defender." One can hardly help regretting that any of these religious animosities were stirred up.

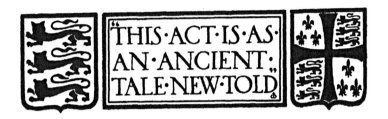

A NCIENT, indeed, is the tale of the Coronation
of the Sovereigns of England in Westminster
Abbey: almost as ancient as the very kingdom
itself, and in very truth as ancient as that
venerable and famous historic church, before whose
altar, after an interval of sixty-four years, this act
is once again to be unfolded, to arouse the interest
and quicken the enthusiasm of millions of British
people the world over. The tale will lose nothing
in popular interest, by reason of its antiquity.

The first coronation of a king of England in
Westminster Abbey took place on Christmas Day
of the year 1066; the last, and one of the most
memorable, on June 28th of the year 1838. The
crowning of King Edward the Seventh and Queen
Alexandra is appointed to be held, as all now
know, in June of this present year of grace 1902
—a succession of events in England's history
continuing in unbroken sequence from the first of
her Norman kings to the seventh of the House of

" THE PLACE WHERE RESTETH THE HOLY BODIE AND RELIQUES OF THE
GLORIOUS KING AND CONFESSOR, ST. EDWARD."

III

The Coronation of Edward VII

Hanover; a period embracing, that is to say, more than eight hundred years, within which period all the sovereigns of England, without exception, have been crowned in Westminster Abbey.

"The place where I was crowned and anointed King; the place also of the common sepulture of the Kings of this Realm, where, within the same, and among the same kings, resteth the holy bodie and reliques of the Glorious King and Confessor, St. Edward, and divers others of our Noble progenitors." Thus in brief is summed up the deep and abiding national interest, the imperishable fame, that belongs to the place where that ancient tale, now in the mouth of many, is presently to be new told before the people. The words quoted appear in the "will" of that king who gave to Westminster Abbey one of its most beautiful parts, that splendid Tudor structure which still bears the name of Henry the Seventh's Chapel. Among that monarch's "noble progenitors," some wrote of it with no less kingly regard and affection : King Edward the Third, for example, as "the Peculiar chapel of our principal Palace, in which We and Our ancestors received our Coronation, and all other Royal honours"; King Edward the

An Ancient Tale New Told

Fourth, as a building which is placed "in the forefront of the world of England . . . of ever-present interest to all of English race . . . founded by our ancestors, consecrated by the Blessed Apostle St. Peter, and distinguished by the tomb of the most saintly Edward, King and Confessor." In the year 1066 (as we have said), William the Conqueror was crowned, close to that tomb; and very near to it every successive king or queen of England— Norman and Plantagenet, Lancaster and York, Tudor, Stuart, and Hanoverian—from that day to this, has received the rite of coronation.

*   *   *   *   *

From the popular, or purely spectacular, point of view, the Pageant and Ceremony of a Coronation in England consists of the scene in Westminster Abbey, and the scene in London Streets; the actual rite and ceremony, that is to say, of the Coronation itself, and the State Procession of the Sovereign to and from Westminster and Buckingham Palace. Time was, when the ancient usage in England was this: Early on the day of the Coronation, sometimes the day before, the Sovereign with all his heralds, judges, councillors, lords, and great dignitaries rode in state, from London's ancient palace and fortress

The Coronation of Edward VII

within the walls, for centuries known as the Tower of London, to that hardly less ancient palace, once adjoining the Abbey at Westminster; or in times less remote, to that once sumptuous town-residence of Wolsey, seized at the cardinal's downfall by Henry the Eighth, originally named York House, and finally the King's palace of Whitehall. Of these regal cavalcades, the last and most imposing was that which passed through London—by way of Tower Hill, Cornhill, Cheapside, St. Paul's, Ludgate, Fleet Street, and the Strand—to Whitehall on April 23rd, 1661, the day when Charles the Second was crowned. His brother and successor, James the Second, when he came to the throne, ordered an estimate to be prepared by his Privy Council, of the cost of such a procession. It was found

An Ancient Tale New Told

that it would amount to something like £50,000 —
a very considerable sum of money in those times.
Being of an economical turn of mind, and not
knowing perhaps how soon he might be in need
of such a sum for his own personal purposes,
James saved that amount on. the city pageant
and spent it on jewels for his wife.

James the Second's example, as regards omitting
the State procession from the Tower to Westminster,
was followed by all his successors in turn. There
is no reason for supposing that his present Majesty,
King Edward the Seventh, will find it convenient
(even if it were to-day possible) to revive the more
ancient usage of so many of his predecessors, of
sojourning for a night in the Constable's lodgings
of his Majesty's Tower of London, merely for the
sake of gratifying the taste for sight-seeing of
some of his subjects. In point of fact, the Royal
Proclamation, made in London on June 28th, 1901,
practically dispenses with "many ancient Customs
and Usages of this Realm," in respect of the
Coronation ceremonies, including, we may be sure,
that of the old-time procession of the Sovereign
from the Tower to Westminster. The Tower has
little modern accommodation to tempt King Edward,

The Coronation of Edward VII

or for that matter any other King, to linger for many hours within its precincts—unless perchance it should be in the hospitable mess-room of the officers of the Brigade of Guards.

Lord Macaulay, incidentally referring to the parsimony, or as some might term it, the shrewdness, not to say "slimness," of James the Second: Lord Macaulay adds some "Whiggish" and snappish remarks, which possibly some of us of to-day may yet be found to agree with: "Sums which well employed, would have afforded exquisite gratification to a large part of the nation, were squandered on an exhibition, to which only three or four thousand privileged persons were admitted. At length the old practice was partially revived. On the day of the Coronation of Queen Victoria, there was a procession in which many deficiencies might be noted, but which was seen with interest and delight by half a million of her subjects, and which undoubtedly gave far greater pleasure, and called forth far greater enthusiasm, than the more costly display which was witnessed by a select circle within Westminster Abbey." Comparatively few persons are privileged to witness the interesting scene of the Coronation within the Abbey itself.

An Ancient Tale New Told

The State Procession, on the other hand, may be viewed by hundreds of thousands of spectators. The longer the line of Route finally chosen by the King, in going to and returning from Westminster, the greater obviously the crowds attracted to London in the hope of seeing it.

State pageants have not been so few and far between in London, of late, as formerly. Within the past fifteen years, for example, we have been witness of two pageants of surpassing splendour and impressiveness : the state processions through London, namely, commemorative of Queen Victoria's jubilees. The coronations of kings, however, are happily not so frequent in England, or even in Europe, as to be familiar in their religious rites, or spectacular parts, to those of us now living. In the course of 836 years, there have been but thirty-six coronations in England, or one on an average in twenty-three years. But, in earlier time, for one reason or another, sovereigns succeeded each other on the English throne at briefer intervals than now. It would be easy to conceive, for example, of a person having been born in the year of Henry the Seventh's accession, the first sovereign of the

The Coronation of Edward VII

House of Tudor (1485), and of having lived to witness the Coronation of the last of that House, Queen Elizabeth (1558); or of a contemporary (say) of Samuel Pepys having lived through the reigns of James I., Charles I., the Commonwealth interval, the reign of Charles II., and to have witnessed the Coronation of James II.—practically five successions all included within a period of eighty-two years. But, it would be accounted a rare incident, to meet with a person who witnessed the Coronation of George IV. and who also witnessed the proclamation at St. James's of Edward the Seventh as King of England—four accessions within a like period of eighty-two years. There has been but one Coronation, as every one knows, in Westminster Abbey in the course of sixty-four years—a fact which should make the present event of exceptional interest to many people; to many thousands of people, at all events, of the United Kingdom and the Colonies.

However divergent the political opinions of some of us may be, we are all more or less interested in pageantry and ceremonial. Your staunchest republican, as history has over and over again shown, is as fond of street processions and parades, of gorgeous uniforms, banners and flags, military music, and the like, as your most thorough-going royalist. Every one relishes a little splendour and display at times. Most persons like to witness regal ceremonies and court functions. Americans, for example, are quite as much interested in such things as ourselves, if we may judge by their splendid appetite for sight-seeing in London. They generally insist on seeing all that is set down in the programme of the London Season. Their ladies go to the Royal "Drawing-rooms" at times; and some few of their men to the Levées. Americans are particularly active in gaining admission to the Houses of Lords and Commons, and seem greatly interested in any official or parliamentary ceremony that there takes place. They are as keen to view the ceremony of the Trooping of the Colour on the Horse Guards' Parade as any average Londoner.

If there be a royal procession to the racecourse at Ascot, you will always find many Americans in the crowd. Their people furnished many thousands of visitors to London on the occasion of the Queen's jubilees, and sent up the prices of windows and seats on the line of route accordingly. The civic

The Coronation of Edward VII

splendour and generous hospitality of the Guildhall and the Mansion House have always been appreciated by Americans, from the days of Washington Irving, N. P. Willis, Nathaniel Hawthorne, and Charles Sumner, to those of George Peabody, Oliver Wendell Holmes, James Russell Lowell, and Chauncey Depew. Charles Sumner in his younger days was never tired of writing to his Boston friends about the grand sights and ceremonies he had witnessed in England. He found a seat in Westminster Abbey at the Coronation of Queen Victoria. Doubtless, a good many of his countrymen will find seats reserved for themselves or their ladies at the Coronation of the King, her son. At all events, we shall hope so. And we may be pardoned perhaps for further hoping, that the great majority will take this book along with them to the Abbey, and there beguile the tedious time of waiting by looking over its pages! It ought to inform some of a good deal they do not know.

In support of that conjecture I need only to again recall a striking passage from the Evidence given by the Very Reverend, the Dean of Westminster (June 13th, 1890) before the Royal Commission on

An Ancient Tale New Told

Westminster Abbey : " There is no doubt," said the Dean, " that William the Conqueror, who always asserted himself to be the heir chosen by the childless King Edward (that is, the Confessor), and lost no opportunity of paying all outward homage to his memory, was crowned close to the grave of his predecessor on Christmas Day, 1066. On or near˙ that spot, every successive king, or queen, who has reigned in England, from that day to this, has received the rite of Coronation." This must be allowed to be a fact of much interest at the present time, confirmed by the high authority of the Dean of Westminster himself. Other facts hardly less so will be found scattered through the pages of this book, which may be expected to serve the two-fold purposes of a guide to the uninformed, and a literary memento of a memorable historic event.

THE COURT OF CLAIMS

EVERYTHING relating to state ceremonials and court functions is regulated by precedent. Turning over the leaves of an old manual of "Rank and Nobility," my eye chanced to fall upon a footnote as follows: "This was the Precedent for the Coronation of his late Majesty, George III., and Queen Charlotte, as well as his present Majesty, George IV.; and is taken from an account published, by his present Majesty's command, by Francis Sandford, Esq., Lancaster Herald of Arms." The matter to which the footnote referred is a full official account, taken from contemporary Privy Council records, of the ceremonial at the Coronation in 1685 of King James the Second and Queen Mary, later noted.

The appointing—as was done in the present instance, by Royal Proclamation of June 28th, 1901 —of a "Court of Claims" by the sovereign, is

The Court of Claims

one of the first acts preliminary to every Coronation in England. Certain persons, noblemen and others, are bound by' tenure of inheritance, or otherwise, to perform various services at that ceremony, and it is their duty to have their pretensions adjudicated upon by the high political, ecclesiastical, and judicial personages whom the King nominates for the purpose. This Court of King Edward VII. was required to sit in the Council Chamber at Whitehall—better known as' the Privy Council Office—five members forming a quorum. It began its deliberations nearly a year before the Coronation was appointed to take place, on Wednesday, July 17th, 1901, namely. Until the beginning of the last century the Coronation had invariably consisted of four distinct ceremonies: the assembling in Westminster Hall, the procession thence to the Abbey, the religious ceremony, and the coronation banquet. William the Fourth was ready (as we have elsewhere said) to dispense with his coronation altogether; but matters were compromised by the omission of everything except the ceremony in the Abbey, preceded, of course, by the Procession through the streets. The late Queen at one time apparently contemplated a revival of all

the ancient ceremonials; but finally it was made
known that the Abbey procession and the Westminster banquet would not take place. King Edward
follows this example, having specially commanded
that the Court of Claims should "exclude from
their consideration such claims that may be submitted to them in respect of rights and services
connected with the parts of the ceremonial heretofore performed in Westminster Hall and with
the Procession." It is the services associated with
the omitted functions—the service of the King's
Champion and many others—which possess most
antiquarian interest. The right to perform them
has not ceased, but remains in abeyance until
again revived. Consequently, the duties of the
Court of Claims were not very onerous.

PRIVY COUNCIL OFFICE,

WHITEHALL,

S.W.

COURT OF CLAIMS.

17th July, 1901.

ADMIT THE BEARER.

BY ORDER.

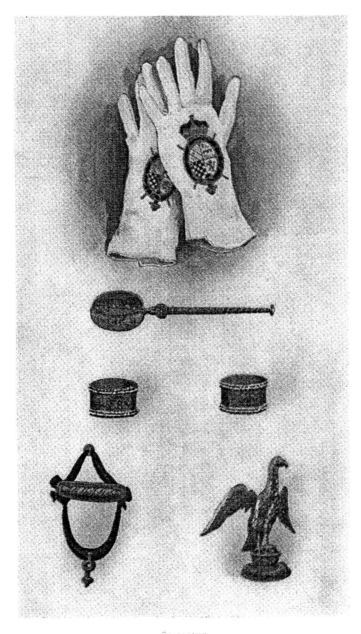

Coronation
Gloves

The   The Anointing Spoon
Spurs
                    Coronation
                    Bracelets

The
Ampullæ
for the Oil of
Anointing

The Court of Claims

With that authority in hand, written in bold hand-writing on a black-bordered, gilt-edged card, and initialled by the gentleman of the Council Office who was so courteous as to grant it, the present writer passed into the Court of Claims on the above-named date at the appointed hour of eleven. One of the lords of the executive committee, who happened to walk through the hall where the writer was waiting, inquired of the doorkeeper : "The place of meeting, I believe, is the old Council Chamber ? " " Yes, my lord," was the reply ; and so in due time some dozen of us in all—gentlemen of the press, officials of the Privy Council, and one or two privileged spectators, walked up the staircase to the old Council Chamber, where in time past Sir Robert Walpole and many another statesman of the Hanoverian sovereigns must have frequently discussed matters of state policy and messages from the King. The committee now assembling were summoned to discuss a message from the King —"These our Letters Pâtent"—"By the King himself, signed with the King's own hand"—as the Clerk of the Crown, standing to the left of the Lord Chancellor, read aloud, from what appeared to be an imposing roll of parchment, doubtless

The Coronation of Edward VII

now duly placed among the archives of the Privy Council, of the first year of the reign of King Edward the Seventh.

With the Reader's permission, I propose to add something about the Council Chamber itself later on. Its old associations moved me more than anything I heard or witnessed, at the first meeting of the "Court of Claims"—its first meeting since the year 1837, when good Queen Victoria first ascended the throne and preparations were being discussed for her own Coronation in the year which was to follow.

Albeit there was a notable, if somewhat meagre company of Peers "all and singular great men" present; to wit, the Lord High Chancellor of England (Earl of Halsbury), the Hereditary Earl Marshal of England (Duke of Norfolk), the Lord President of the Council (Duke of Devonshire), the Lord Chamberlain (Earl of Clarendon), the Chancellor of the Duchy of Lancaster (Lord James of Hereford, who might and would have been, some years ago, Lord High Chancellor of England, but for the waywardness of politics), a Lord of Appeal in Ordinary (Lord Robertson), the Lord Chancellor of Ireland (Lord Ashbourne),

126

The Court of Claims

the Master of the Rolls (Sir Archibald Smith), and Sir Francis Jeune, Judge of the High Court: although "all and singular great men" these personages of State were present in person, the eye searched in vain for any outward or visible tokens of their greatness. Of coat-armour, robes, or coronets bore they none. Save for the crimson cloth furniture of the Council Chamber, there was not a particle of colour to be seen in the place.

Their lordships entered in ordinary morning attire; the Hereditary Earl Marshal of England, Knight of the Most Noble Order of the Garter, etc., etc., in, to our experienced eye, the most ordinary attire of all. It is obvious that Lord Chesterfield's Letters, incidentally touching on the always interesting topic of dress, are of no account with the peerage of England now. Alas, for historic continuity and the ancient traditions of the Court of Claims, that it should so happen that at the very first function (if we may so consider it) connected with the Coronation of King Edward VII., lineal descendant of Norman, and Plantagenet, Houses of Lancaster and York, Tudor, Stuart, and Hanoverian kings, his Majesty's "right trusty and

The Coronation of Edward VII

entirely beloved Cousins and Councillors," should assemble in council in ordinary morning attire! Robes and coronets, at least, might have been looked for ; if not ribbons and orders of knight-hood. But, the common or everyday Bond Street variety of frock-coats! Who cares to see a great officer of state—Hereditary Earl Marshal, Lord Steward, Lord Chamberlain, or the Keeper of the King's Conscience—in a plain frock-coat (we even noticed a "shooting-jacket" among the number) that you or I might buy any day in the Strand for a five-pound note!

Briefly, this "Court of Claims" finds its origin in the ancient prerogatives of the Lord High Steward, who sat judicially . in the. hall of the King's Palace at Westminster, to receive the applications, and decide upon the claims, of all who held lands on the tenure of performing some personal service at the King's Coronation. Thus a *postmortem* inquisition, dated the VIIth year of Edward the Third (1334), speaks of the tenure of the Manor of Scrivelsby Court, Lincolnshire, formerly in possession of the Dymokes, hereditary King's Champions, as follows : "That the Manor of Scrivelsby is holden by Grand Serjeantry to

The Court of Claims

wit, by the service of finding on the day of Coronation an armed knight, who shall prove by his body if need be, that the King is true and rightful heir to the Kingdom." By Act of Parliament (59 George III., c. 46) the ancient trial and battle were abolished altogether ; so that the Champion's lands, after being held with manifest peril for centuries, at last became a peaceable possession of his heirs; and consequently all dispute respecting the crown fully disposed of. The last of the Dymokes, however, in direct line, in the person of Sir Henry Dymoke, died in 1865, so that there is now no hereditary King's Champion of England living, even if his former high and ancient office had not become obsolete—at all events since the reign of George IV. The Manor of Scrivelsby still stands where it did ; but not held now by its interesting old-time tenure. The Barony of Burghley (1571), belonging to the Marquis of Exeter, is held in right of that peer's office of Hereditary Grand Almoner, whose duties anciently were, and still are, to collect and distribute certain moneys at the Coronation from a silver dish, which the Almoner claims for his fee. He was also entitled to the cloth on which the

The Coronation of Edward VII

King walked in procession from the door of Westminster Hall to the Abbey. The office of Chief Butler at the Coronation is hereditary in the Dukes of Norfolk as Earls of Arundel. Lordship of the Isle of Man was formerly also another tenure held of the Kings of England, by some personage presenting the sovereign with two falcons on the day of ·his Coronation. The Duke of Atholl, of George III.'s time, held the manorial rights of the Island by such tenure, which dates from at least Henry IV.'s reign, if not much earlier.

Any stranger casually peeping in at the door on the "Committee of Claims" might have mistaken the great noblemen there foregathered, "right trusty and entirely beloved Cousins and Councillors" of the King, to consider of the King's Coronation, for any half-dozen borough or town councillors, met together to discuss some commonplace question of rates and taxes. When the Clerk of the Crown —all persons being commanded to keep silence— had read the message "by the King himself, signed with the King's own hand"—"Let all persons withdraw" was the sentence forthwith pronounced by the Registrar of the Privy Council. So we all

The Court of Claims

passed out, curious to learn (among other things) what this digression might mean. In a quarter of an hour, we were recalled. Their lordships had been merely discussing procedure.

The Registrar of the Privy Council now proceeded to read out some of the petitions received as follows :

The Earl of Lauderdale, to carry the King's ensigns of war, as hereditary standard-bearer for Scotland.

Henry Scrymgeour Wedderburn, to carry the Royal Standard, as hereditary standard-bearer for Scotland.

The Walker Trustees [whoever these may be], to exercise the office of Usher of the White Rod for Scotland by deputy.

G. T. J. Sotheron-Estcourt, to exercise the duty of Chief Larderer, as owner of the manor of Shipton Moyne.

The Duke of Norfolk, to act as Chief Butler of England.

Mr. Frederick Oddin Taylor, as lord of the manor of Kenninghall, to act as Chief Butler.

The Marquis of Exeter, to exercise the office of Almoner, as possessor of the barony of Burghley.

The Coronation of Edward VII

The Earl of Ancaster and the Marquis of Chol-mondeley, as exercising the office of Lord Great Chamberlain of England, to perform the duties and services thereof. [These claims gave rise to a trial before the House of Lords.]

The Duke of Newcastle, as holder of the manor of Worksop, to provide a glove and support the King's arm.

The Bishop of Durham and the Bishop of Bath and Wells, to support their Majesties at the Coronation.

The Duke of Somerset, to carry the Orb.

The Earl of Erroll, to walk as Lord High Constable of Scotland, and to have a silver bâton tipped with gold.

Robert Henry Potter, nature of services not stated.

The Dean and Chapter of Westminster, to instruct the King and Queen in the Rites and Ceremonies, and to assist the Archbishop of Canterbury, and to have cloth, etc., for fees.

Lord Grey de Ruthyn, to carry the golden spurs.

Lyon King of Arms and the Heralds and Pursuivants of Scotland, to be present at the Coronation.

The Court of Claims

The borough of Camberwell, to be represented at the Coronation.

Colonel C. G. Brown, as baron and jurat of Fordwich, to bear the canopy over the King and Queen—a privilege accorded to the barons of the Cinque Ports.

The Registrar also said notice of other petitions had been received, including the following:

Lord Hastings and Lord Grey de Ruthyn, to carry the great spurs.

The scholars of St. Peter's College, Westminster, (Westminster School), to be present at and take formal part in the Coronation.

The Earl of Shrewsbury and Talbot, (1) to carry a white staff as Lord High Steward of Ireland; and (2) to provide a glove for the King's right hand and support his hand whilst holding the sceptre.

Sir Windham Carmichael Anstruther, to exercise the office of Hereditary Grand Carver for Scotland.

The Duke of Buccleuch, as Gold Stick for Scotland, to ride by his Majesty's carriage.

The Marquis of Winchester, to carry the Cap of Maintenance.

133

The Coronation of Edward VII

We are almost afraid to mention a brief observation on all these matters, which we overheard pass from one gentleman to another, in the ante-room of the Council Chamber: "Ridiculous, but somewhat amusing!" It seemed to us that some of their lordships themselves might have felt not indisposed to agree, had it not been that they were present as principals in the proceedings, rather than as spectators. There was a good hearty laugh from one of the peers present, when all was ended. Truly, it does seem a trifle ridiculous that the Lord High Chancellor of England should be troubled with a point, as to whether some distinguished gentleman is to exercise the office of "Hereditary Grand Carver for Scotland"—with probably no baron of beef anywhere forthcoming worthy of his skill; or whether another gentleman is to carry a silver bâton tipped with gold; or a third a white staff; or another is " to bear the canopy over the King and Queen "—doubtless greatly to his own discomfiture, since most regal canopies would require at least six or eight gentlemen to support them. However, honour to whom honour is due, and let all things be done decently and in order. We hope that every claim

The Court of Claims

was held good, and will be allowed on the day
of Coronation.

*   *   *   *   *

The Council Chamber where the committee sat
is interesting for more reasons than one. It is of
respectable antiquity, its progenitor having been
born, according to our reckoning, some time in
the days of Wolsey's chancellorship. It smacks
of regality, of history, and of law ; topics which
generally command the interest of a good many.
During a long and intimate acquaintance with
this cheerful wilderness of London, I have met
with but one person of the commonalty, or, more
properly speaking, perhaps, general public, who
could say that he had entered the Council Chamber,
Whitehall—and he, as a matter of course, was an
American ! Truly, the American knows much more
of London, than the Londoner himself. There can
hardly be a place of any interest in London hidden
from us that has not been revealed to him, whose
insatiable curiosity and spirited enterprise in searching
out and looking up things, surely entitle him to
the distinction of a master's degree in the art of
sight-seeing.

I doubt if one Londoner in a hundred knows

135

The Coronation of Edward VII

the precise whereabouts of the Council Chamber,
and what business is generally transacted there.
To satisfy a not unreasonable curiosity at this
particular time, let us at once say, that the Privy
Council Office is within a stone's throw of the
First Lord of the Treasury's official residence in
Downing Street, one of the oldest streets remaining in Whitehall, if not quite the oldest. The
historic chamber itself is mostly reserved now to
the occasional meetings of the "Judicial Committee
of the Privy Council," direct successors (so a
learned and courteous official of the Privy Council
assures us) of the far more famous—or infamous—
"Star Chamber," anciently attached to the Courts
at Westminster. Its reputation was such that the
legend, "Abandon hope all ye who enter here,"
might much more aptly have been inscribed over
its narrow oaken doorway, than the golden chiselled
star, emblem of better promise, which in fact
appeared there. In the legal annals of England,
no court ever earned a more evil reputation than
the Star Chamber of Westminster adjoining the
Abbey, if we exclude that of the Western circuit
of the "Bloody Assize," presided over by Judge
Jeffreys.

The Court of Claims

Not to know one's Star Chamber, so to say, is to admit but a very insufficient knowledge of English history. Its proceedings in the days of Stuarts generally ended in the cropping of ears, branding of foreheads, the public pillory, exorbitant money fines, and close imprisonment, not seldom for life. Its iniquitous and cruel sentences roused the indignation of the citizens of London, and had not a little to do with the outbreak of the Civil War and the execution of King Charles the First in front of the banqueting-house over yonder. Originally founded by Henry VIII. in the old palace of the kings at Westminster, it was continued·as a court of law till the seventeenth year of Charles I. The judges of the court were the Privy Council. Its most famous prosecution was that of Prynne, a barrister of Lincoln's Inn, by the notorious Attorney-General Noy. In the year 1641, the Star Chamber was abolished by statute. It really took the name (as we believe) from its ceiling of oak ornamented, among other devices, with golden stars. Its sittings were held in Term time, once a week at the least, usually on Wednesdays and Fridays, from nine till eleven ; the Lord Chancellor, the lords and others of the Privy

The Coronation of Edward VII

Council, and the Lord Chief Justice of England constituting the court. Somewhat similar arrangements hold good now in respect of the Judicial Committee of Privy Council, except that the judges of the High Court of Justice are increased in number. The two Archbishops, Canterbury and York, and the Bishop of London sit in appeals under the Clergy Discipline Act.

The most interesting reminiscences of the Council Chamber are its records kept in an office below. The gentleman who had them in charge was good enough to unlock the bookcase where they are carefully bestowed and to hand us a weighty volume bearing on its back in gold lettering the words "Elizabeth and Mary, 1558-1559." It was bound in ancient leather, curiously tooled, and strengthened at back with leathern straps, stitched with catgut. The paper and handwriting are in as good state of preservation as when first made, and penned. The first page reported a deliberation of Queen Elizabeth's Privy Council at the palace at Greenwich. The records run (we doubt, however, if in unbroken sequence) from those days to the reign of her Majesty Queen Victoria. My attention was attracted to a volume

The Court of Claims

of Charles the First's, maybe recording the abolition of the famous, or infamous, Star Chamber, of
which, as the gentleman in charge of these interesting records reminded us with some share of
pardonable satisfaction—"We of this office are the
direct successors."

THE ARMS OF QUEEN ELIZABETH.

The Day Proclaimed.

THE Day of the Coronation was announced in accordance with old-time regulation by Royal Proclamation in London and elsewhere; in the present instance six months in advance of the actual date fixed. To students of history, the document will be interesting, not less as a reminder of the lengthy continuity of the English monarchy, than as embodying some of the terms of similar State-papers published by the sovereign in times long past. For example the ancient phrase in which the Proclamation summons "all persons of what rank or quality soever they be," having service to render at the Coronation, to attend "in all respects furnished and appointed, as to so great a solemnity appertaineth," is in itself a vivid reminder of the unique heritage of long tradition, symbolised in the celebration in the second year of the twentieth century of a new succession to the British Crown. That crown belongs to the supreme head of an Empire more extensive and wonderful by far, as

The Day Proclaimed

it now is, than any over which a Monarch, whether of ancient or modern times, was ever before summoned to become Ruler.

In the second week of December, 1901, the following was published in a supplement of the official *London Gazette* :—

"By the KING.

"A PROCLAMATION.

"*For appointing a Day for the Celebration of the Solemnity of the Coronation of Their Majesties. EDWARD*, R.I.

"WHEREAS, by Our Royal Proclamation, bearing date the twenty-sixth day of June last, We did (amongst other things) publish and declare Our Royal intention to celebrate the Solemnity of Our Royal Coronation and of the Coronation of Our dearly beloved Consort the Queen, upon a day of June next to be thereafter determined, at Our Palace at Westminster ; and whereas We have resolved by the favour and blessing of Almighty God to celebrate the said Solemnity upon Thursday, the twenty-sixth day of June next : We do, by this Our Royal Proclamation, give notice thereof, and We do hereby strictly charge and command all Our loving subjects whom it may concern, that all persons, of what rank or quality soever they be, who either upon Our Letters to them directed, or by reason of their offices and tenures, or otherwise, are to do any service at the time of Our Coronation, do duly give their attendance at the said Solemnity on Thursday, the twenty-sixth day of June next, in all respects furnished and appointed as to so great a Solemnity appertaineth and answerable to the dignities and places which every one of them respectively holdeth and enjoyeth, and of this they or any of them are not to fail, as they will answer the contrary at their perils, unless upon special reasons by Ourself under Our hand to be allowed, We shall dispense with any of their services or attendances:

" Provided always, and We do further by this Our Royal Proclamation signify and declare, that nothing herein contained shall be construed to change or alter Our Royal determination as more fully declared in Our Royal Proclamation bearing date the twenty-sixth day of June last, whereby We did signify it to be Our Royal Will and Pleasure, upon the occasion of this Our Coronation, to dispense with that part of the Ceremonial which heretofore took place in Westminster Hall, and that part thereof which consisted of the Procession.

" Given at Our Court at *Saint James's*, this tenth day of *December*, in the year of our Lord one thousand nine hundred and one, and in the first year of Our Reign.

" GOD save the KING."

Peers Peeresses and other People

L ONDONERS City-wards travelling, well enough
know by sight the Heralds' College in Queen
Victoria Street: a picturesque brick building with
forecourt, reminiscent historically of Tudor days, and
architecturally of those of the Stuarts. It was, in
fact, built after " the great Fire of London," as we
still continue to name that event. " A gorgeous
idea of colours," as Leigh Hunt suggests, falls on
the mind of him who happens to recall his
English history in passing it. Not many of us
have had the privilege of seeing in state-dress the
Kings at Arms—Garter, Clarencieux, and Norroy—
who preside over its mysteries. A story is told
—a story too good, we fear, to be true; but
related on the authority of Langton, Dr. Johnson's
life-long friend—that an Irish King at Arms,
who waited upon an Irish bishop to summon
him to the national Parliament in Dublin, and
being dressed, as the ceremony then required,
in his heraldic attire, so mystified the bishop's

143

servant with his appearance, that not knowing
what to make of it, and carrying off but a
confused notion of his title, he announced him to
his master thus : " My lord, here is the King of
Trumps ! "

Garter, principal King at Arms, is one of the
most fantastic and gorgeously attired officials of
any Court.   His state-dress, only worn on great
occasions, reminds one of nothing so much as that
of the pictured kings in a pack of playing-cards : a
frock, or tabard, of rich crimson and gold, on which
is emblazoned, back and front, the royal quarterings
of the United Kingdom—the lions of England,
the " ruddy lion rampt in gold " of Scotland, the
golden harp of Ireland.   The other so-named kings
in English heraldry, associated with Garter, are
Clarencieux (a title of Norman origin) of the
south, and Norroy (Nord Roi) of the north.   The
heralds associated with these three are Lancaster,
Somerset, Richmond, etc., only less gorgeously
caparisoned than the Kings at Arms ; and then
there are the four pursuivants (attendants or
messengers) severally entitled Rouge Croix, Rouge
Dragon, Portcullis, and Blue Mantle, with hues as
lively, and appellations as quaint, as the attendants

Peers, Peeresses, and other People

on a fairy court. All these historic officials of England have their place in the King's Coronation, under their chief, the Earl Marshal of England, the Duke of Norfolk. For gorgeousness of dress, mysteriousness of origin, and in fact for similarity of origin (a knave being nothing less than an esquire), a knave of cards in design and colour is not unlike a herald in his tabard.

By the way, the unlearned generally attribute to the Royal shield, three Leopards! But these (so-called) "leopards," two of which William the Conqueror took for the Royal arms and to which Henry II. added the third, are in fact "leo-pards" or "leos-pardés," that is to say, lions *passant guardant*; one being the ancient device of Normandy, the other that of Poitou, and the third the Lion of Aquitaine.

These reminiscences of bygone times, of kings and queens, Plantagenet, York and Lancaster, and Tudor, of bannered halls (such as we have in Henry VII.'s Chapel of Westminster Abbey and St. George's Chapel, Windsor), of processions of chivalry, and of the fields of Crécy and Poictiers, and of the famous meeting on the Field of the

The Coronation of Edward VII

Cloth of Gold : these historic reminiscences recall the times of vizored knights distinguished by their coats and crests. A coat of arms, so called, is in heraldry nothing but a pictorial representation of the knight himself, from whom the wearer, or bearer, is descended. The shield, so named, supposes his body ; there is the helmet for his head, with the crest upon it ; the flourish is the mantle ; and he stands upon the ground of his "motto," or moral pretension. The "supporters," if he be noble, or of a particular class of knighthood, are thought to be the pages that waited upon him, designated by the curiously fantastic dresses of a lion, bear, leopard, stag, unicorn, etc., which they originally sometimes wore, or are supposed to have worn. Heraldry is full of colour and imagery, and attracts the fancy like a book of pictures. One might spend half an hour not unprofitably, in looking over the pages of Debrett's " Peerage and Baronetage," and studying some of the coats of arms, mottoes, and supporters of the ancient aristocracy of England. Many a forgotten, but interesting and eventful, lesson in history might be thus revived.

*　　*　　*　　*　　*

Not to wander too far from the point ; some

Peers, Peeresses, and other People

have supposed the late Lord Beaconsfield (Benjamin Disraeli, of that name) to have been an aristocrat of the aristocrats. Read what he puts into the mouth of one of the personages of his books.* He wrote the book we refer to, it is right to add, before he became Peer of the Realm himself; but the quotation we append probably truly expressed his own personal opinion on such matters :—

"'Ancient lineage! I never heard of a Peer with an ancient lineage. The real old families of this country are to be found among the Peasantry. The gentry, too, may lay some claim to old blood. I can point you out Saxon families in this county [maybe his own county of Buckingham] who can trace their pedigrees beyond the Conquest. I know of some Norman gentlemen whose forefathers undoubtedly came over with the Conqueror. But, a peer with an ancient lineage is to me quite a novelty. No, no; the thirty years of the wars of the Roses freed us from those gentlemen. After the battle of Tewkesbury a Norman baron was almost as rare a being, as a wolf is now.

* Millbank, in "Coningsby.'

147

The Coronation of Edward VII

"'I have always understood,' said Coningsby, 'that our peerage was the finest in Europe.'

"'For themselves,' said Millbank, 'and the heralds who paint their carriages. But, I go to facts. When Henry VII. called his first Parliament* there were only twenty-nine temporal peers to be found; and even some of those took their seats illegally, for they had been attainted. Of those twenty-nine, not five remain, and they, as the Howards, for instance, are not Norman nobility. We owe the English peerage to three sources: the spoliation of the Church; the open and flagrant sale of its honours by the elder Stuarts; and the borough-mongering of our own times. Those are the three main sources of the existing peerages of England, and in my opinion disgraceful ones. But I must apologise for this frankness in speaking to an aristocrat.'

"'Oh, by no means, sir; I like discussion.'

"'And where will you find your natural aristocracy?' asked Coningsby.

"'Among those men whom the nation recognises as the most eminent for virtues, talents, and property, and, if you please, birth and standing in

* November 1485.

148

Peers, Peeresses, and. other People

the land. They guide opinion, and therefore they govern. I am no leveller. I look upon an artificial equality as equally pernicious with a factitious aristocracy; both depressing the energies and checking the enterprise of a nation. I like a man to be free, really free; free in his industry as well as in his body. What is the use of Habeas Corpus, if a man may not use his hands and brains when he is out of prison?'"

Thus the late Benjamin Disraeli, Lord Beaconsfield, Knight of the most Noble Order of the Garter, who used at least one of his hands, and all his brains, to notable purpose. No application of "Habeas Corpus" either fettered or aided him. He was far too clever ever to fall within its cognisance. And, he came of the People.

Walter Savage Landor puts much the same thoughts into the mind of Andrew Marvell, in his "Imaginary Conversation" with Bishop Parker: "It is probable that many among the poor and abject are of very ancient families, and particularly in our county [York], where the contests of the York and Lancaster broke down in many places

The Coronation of Edward VII

the high and powerful. Some of us may look back six or seven centuries and find a stout ruffian at the beginning ; but the great ancestors of the pauper, who must be somewhere, may stand perhaps far beyond."

* * * * *

The great Officers of State of the King's household—each of whom plays an important part in arranging the details of the King's Coronation—are the Lord Chamberlain, the Lord Steward, and the Master of the Horse. We may as well state their respective duties in the King's household. The first-named has the care of all the officers and servants belonging to the King's chambers, except those belonging to his bedchamber, who are under an officer named the Groom of the Stole—from "stole," a robe, or better derived from a verb meaning "to array." The Lord Chamberlain (not to be confounded with the Lord Great Chamberlain, a high official personage of the House of Lords) has the oversight of the officers of the wardrobe, of tents (as in olden time), of revels, music, comedians—an officer is still entrusted with the duty of licensing stage-plays, called "the Examiner of Plays," and the Lord Chamberlain himself has

jurisdiction over certain of the London theatres—
of handicrafts and artisans ; and, although a layman,
the Lord Chamberlain has the oversight also of all
the King's heralds, chaplains, physicians, and apothe-
caries. It is his duty to inspect the charges of
coronations (but the Cabinet usually has something
to say about these, first of all), marriages, public
entries, cavalcades, and funerals; also of all
furniture—such, at all events, used to be the case ;
it may not, however, be so now—in the House of
Lords, and the rooms of access to the King.
The state palaces of Windsor Castle, Buckingham
Palace, St. James's, may be said to be generally
under his charge ; and all functions, such as Drawing-
rooms and Levées, State Balls and State Concerts,
he, in the main, oversees.

The Lord Steward has the estate of the household
entirely committed to his care ; and all his commands
in this particular are to be obeyed. His authority
reaches over all officers and servants of the King's
house, except those of his chamber and chapel. The
office at Buckingham Palace where the accounts of
the household are kept is still known as "the Board of
Green Cloth." The Treasurer, Comptroller, Master,
Paymaster, etc., are under his control ; as also

are all affairs of the kitchen and cellars. At State Banquets it is he who calls the toast to the King.

The Master of the Horse has the charge and government of the Royal Mews, the stables and horses of the sovereign. He has also power over the equerries, pages, footmen, grooms, coachmen, farriers, smiths, etc., etc., and all other trades connected with the stables. In State Processions, he rides next behind the King. He has the privilege of applying to his own use one coachman, four footmen, and six grooms in the King's pay, and wearing the royal livery—which, by the way, is scarlet, faced with blue and edged with gold.

* * * * *

It may interest those privileged to be present in the Abbey to know how they may discover one Peer or Peeress from another Peer or Peeress by the glory of his or her apparel worn at the Coronation " of their Most Sacred Majesties King Edward the Seventh and Queen Alexandra."

The robe or mantle of the Peers is of crimson velvet, edged with miniver, the cape furred with miniver pure, and powdered with bars or rows of ermine (*i.e.*, narrow pieces of black fur), according

Peers, Peeresses, and other People

to their degree. Thus : Barons wear two rows ; Viscounts, two rows and a half ; Earls, three rows ; Marquises, three rows and a half ; Dukes, four rows. The mantles or robes are worn over full Court dress, uniform, or regimentals. The coronets are of silver gilt ; the caps of crimson velvet turned up with ermine, with a gold tassel on the top ; and no jewels or precious stones are permitted to be used in the coronets, or " counterfeit pearls instead of silver balls." Such is the Earl Marshal's order.

The coronet of a baron has on its circle or rim six silver balls at equal distances ; the coronet of a viscount has on its circle sixteen silver balls ; the coronet of an earl, in the like position, eight silver balls, raised upon points, with gold strawberry-leaves between the points ; the coronet of a marquis, in the like, four gold strawberry-leaves and four silver balls alternately, the latter a little raised on points above the rim ; and the coronet of a duke has on the circle eight gold strawberry-leaves.

All Peeresses who attend wear the robes or mantles appertaining to their respective ranks over the usual full Court dress required of ladies. The robes of the peeresses are, if anything, more effective, ladies

The Coronation of Edward VII

may be satisfied to learn, than those of the peers. The entire dress is carried out in rich crimson velvet, bordered with miniver. First, there is the kirtle of the velvet opening over a petticoat of white satin and lace, of which the details may be slightly varied if the selected colour and material are alike. The edges of the kirtle are waved and bordered with miniver ; and it falls gracefully back on each side, nearly meeting at the waist, but widening out well at the feet. The corsage is cut with a plastron of white miniver reaching from the decolletage to the waist, whilst the sleeves reach the elbow, and are cut and slashed and edged with fur, and there are two narrow bands of fur above the slashings, which are deemed to be strictly regulation. The sleeves are finished with full frills of lace. The long train hangs from the shoulders. It is lined with white silk and bordered with white miniver, which varies in width according to the rank of the wearer. The length of the train also varies in the same manner. For whereas a duchess is entitled to the full glory of two yards upon the ground, the marchioness may only have one and three-quarters, and a baroness one yard. The official regulations are as follows :—

Peers, Peeresses, and other People

The robe or mantle of a Baroness is of crimson velvet; the cape furred with miniver pure, and powdered with two bars or rows of ermine (*i.e.*, narrow pieces of black fur). The said mantle is edged round with miniver pure two inches in breadth, and the train to be three feet on the ground; the coronet according to her degree—viz., a rim or circle with six pearls (represented by silver balls) upon the same, not raised upon points.

The robe or mantle of a Viscountess is like that of a Baroness, only the cape is powdered with two rows and a half of ermine, the edging of the mantle two inches as before, and the train a yard and a quarter ; the coronet according to her degree—viz., a rim or circle with pearls (represented by silver balls) thereon, sixteen in number, and not raised upon points.

The robe or mantle of a Countess as before, only the cape is powdered with three rows of ermine, the edging three inches in breadth, and the train a yard and a half. The coronet is composed of eight pearls (represented by silver balls) raised upon points or rays, with small strawberry-leaves between, above the rim.

The Coronation of Edward VII

The robe or mantle of a Marchioness as before, only the cape is powdered with three rows and a half of ermine, the edging four inches in breadth, the train a yard and three-quarters. The coronet is composed of four strawberry-leaves and four pearls (represented by silver balls) raised upon points of the same height as the leaves, alternately, above the rim.

The robe or mantle of a Duchess as before, only the cape is powdered with four rows of ermine, the edging five inches broad, the train two yards. The coronet is composed of eight strawberry leaves, all of equal height, above the rim.

The caps of all the coronets are of crimson velvet, turned up with ermine, with a tassel of gold on the top.

All these matters are more or less interesting; interesting in much the same way that old books, old castles, old churches, and the like are interesting. They speak to us of the Past. They serve to remind us of other men, other times, and other manners in old England. You and I, dear Reader, as "the great week-day preacher"* once wrote in one of the many sermons he scattered through

* Thackeray.

Peers, Peeresses, and other People

his works; you and I know the ·exact value of
heraldic designs—of coat-armour, strips of ermine,
coronets, and the rest. "We know that though
the greatest pleasure of all is to act like a gentleman, it is a pleasure, nay a merit, to be one; to
come of an old stock, to have an honourable
pedigree, to be able to say that centuries back our
fathers had gentle blood, and to us transmitted
the same. There is good in Gentility. The man
who questions it is envious, or a coarse dullard
not able to perceive the differences between high
breeding and low. . . . In the matter of gentlemen,
democrats say, 'Psha! give us one of nature's
gentlemen and hang your aristocrats.' And so,
indeed, Nature does make some gentlemen—a
few here and there. But, Art makes most: good
birth, that is good, handsome, well-formed fathers
and mothers, good home training, good food,
good education, cleanly and wholesome lives,
few cares, pleasant easy habits of life, and
luxuries not too great or enervating, but only
refining: a course of these going on for a few
generations are the best gentlemen-makers in the
world, and beat Nature hollow."

Few would dispute these opinions, even when

The Coronation of Edward VII

weighed against the following from the pen of
one of greater authority than Thackeray :—

> "From lowest place when virtuous things proceed,
> The place is dignified by the doer's deed;
> Where great additions swell, and virtues none,
> It is a dropsied honour; good alone
> Is good without a name.
>   . . . That is honour's scorn,
> Which challenges itself as honour's born,
> And is not like the sire : Honours thrive,
> When rather from our acts we them derive
> Than our fore-goers."

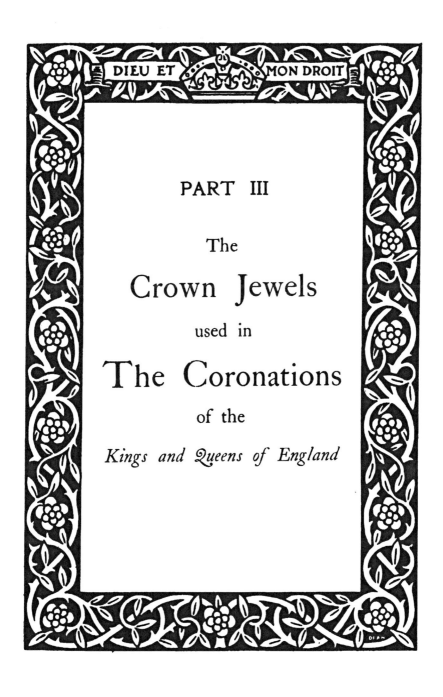

DIEU ET MON DROIT

PART III

The

Crown Jewels

used in

The Coronations

of the

Kings and Queens of England

The Regalia of England

SOME persons would not wish to see even the "mock-pearls" of History trampled under foot. It may be just as well, however, to remind admirers of such pearls that the present Regalia of England is not that consecrated by the religious rites and observances of Coronations prior to the reign of Charles II. The crown jewels now occasionally used possess no claim to be considered even copies of the ancient Regalia which, as students of English history know, were taken out of the "Treasury Chest" of Westminster Abbey, and later sold by order of the Parliament of Cromwell. The story runs, that to Henry Martin was entrusted "the welcome task" of breaking open the huge iron chest in the ancient chapel of the "Treasury," where the crown jewels had been mostly preserved for some six hundred years. It is said that Martin dragged out the crown, the sceptre, orb, and coronation robes, and put them on George

The Coronation of Edward VII

Withers the poet, "who did first trail about the town with a stately garb, and afterwards with a thousand apish and ridiculous antics exposed those sacred ornaments to contempt and laughter." This most probably is a mock-pearl of history; for if so displayed in the streets on the person of George Withers the poet, it is amazing that the crown jewels ever fell into the custody of Parliament. They were much more likely to have been stolen.

From the days of the early kings of England down to the time of the Commonwealth, the "Treasury," once so named as containing the Regalia, had been in the custody of the Deans and Chapter of Westminster. On January 23rd, 1643, a motion was made in the House of Commons that the Dean, Sub-Dean, and Prebendaries should be required to deliver up the keys; and the question put, whether, upon the refusal of the keys, the doors of the "Treasury" should be broken open? So strong, it would seem, was the deference shown to the ancient rights of the Chapter that, even in those excited times, the question was lost by 58 votes against 37; and when the doors were finally forced, it was only permitted to be done on the understanding that an inventory should be taken, new

162

Salt Spoon

State Salt Cellars

Sacramental
Flagon

State
Salt Cellar

The Regalia of England

locks put on the doors, and nothing removed till upon further order of the House of Commons; and this was carried by a vote of 42 against 41.

Cromwell's Parliament in fact got hold of the Regalia, and unfortunately for us of to-day who find an interest in antiquarian matters, the six-centuries old Crown Jewels of Plantagenets and Tudors were broken up and sold, and perforce we have now to be content with the sight of a Regalia only some 258 years old. Neither Charles the Second nor James the Second appear to have been greatly disturbed by their loss. James contrived to find and lay out more than £100,000 in dressing his Queen and saved some thousands of pounds more, so history says, in omitting the time-honoured procession from the Tower to Westminster.

The Regalia of Charles II.'s reign were, and are yet, called by the old names, and though now permanently kept in the Tower of London, are still, by a shadowy connection with the past, deposited in the Dean of Westminster's custody on the eve of the Coronation, either in the Jerusalem Chamber or in one of the private closets in his Library. Among the other time-honoured privileges of the Deans (it may be mentioned), derived from those

The Coronation of Edward VII

of their ancient predecessors, the Abbots of
Westminster, is that of instructing or directing the
sovereign in the details of the Coronation Service.
Of all the clergy of England, the Dean and Canons
of Westminster alone are privileged to stand by
the side of the Prelates in administering the historic
rites. The Dean has still the charge of the " Liber
Regalis " referred to (p. 232), containing the ancient
" order " of the service; and the duty (we believe)
devolves upon him, and not on the bishops present,
of consecrating the sacred oil used in the ceremony
of anointing.

*   *   *   *   *

Turning sharp round to the right, as you pass
under the ancient gateway of the Bloody Tower,
over against the lodgings of the Keeper of the
Jewels, which stand above Traitor's Gate, is the
Wakefield Tower. In a small apartment of that
building is his Majesty's Jewel House where the
Crown Regalia is kept—a very splendid display
of rich gold and jewels, crowns, sceptres, orbs,
swords, dishes, flagons, salt-cellars, sacramental
plate, maces, state trumpets, used at the Coronation of the kings and queens of England. The
public was first permitted to view these jewels

The Regalia of England

of state in Charles II.'s reign, by a kind of
dereliction of duty on the part of their then
custodian, an officer formerly known as the Master
of the Jewel House. He was a court functionary
of some importance, being esteemed "the first
Knight Bachelor of England," having the appoint-
ment of "Goldsmith to the King" in his gift.
His profits and perquisites were originally very
considerable; but when Charles II. came to his
own, the Master of the Jewel House (Sir William
Talbot) got little enough for his portion. In brief,
his profits had to be made the best way he could.
So he allowed his confidential servant to take fees
for showing the Regalia to strangers, which fees
went into his own pocket. When that servant died
an offer of five hundred old broad-pieces of gold
was made to Sir William for the place. From which
fact we may conclude, that both master and servant
made a tolerably good thing by surreptitiously showing the Regalia to those of the citizens who were
curious to see them. The old Jewel House, which
was originally a strong chamber in the Martin
Tower, was not open to the public, save on payment of a somewhat excessive fee, till somewhere
about the year 1842, when the Regalia was removed

to another stronghold near where the officers' mess-room now stands. That in its turn gave place to the present chamber in the Wakefield Tower, where the Crown Jewels may be viewed by any one on "free days," and on any other day on payment of a small fee.

With the Reader's permission, I now propose to describe the Crown Regalia, of which we publish full-page illustrations in colours.

*   *   *   *   *

THE IMPERIAL CROWN in the centre was made for the Coronation of Queen Victoria. It is composed of a cap of purple velvet, enclosed by hoops of silver, richly dight with gems in the form shown in the illustration. The arches rising almost to a point, instead of being depressed, are covered with pearls, and are surmounted by an orb of brilliants. Upon this is placed a Maltese or cross *pattée* of brilliants. Four crosses and four *fleurs-de-lis* surmount the circlet, all composed of diamonds, the front cross containing the "inestimable sapphire," of the purest and deepest azure, more than two inches long, and an inch broad ; and, in the circlet beneath it, is a rock ruby of great size and exquisite colour, which tradition says was worn by

The Regalia of England

the Black Prince at the battle of Cressy, and by Henry V. at the battle of Agincourt. The circlet is enriched with diamonds, emeralds, sapphires, and rubies. The crown was altered from one constructed expressly for the Coronation of King George IV. The superb diadem then weighed 5½ lb., and was worn by the King on his return in procession from the Abbey to the Hall at Westminster; but on arriving at the Hall, he exchanged this crown for one about half the weight, made by the then Crown Jewellers, Messrs. Rundell and Bridge, for the occasion, the jewels being lent for the purpose. This lighter crown was broken up immediately afterwards.

THE OLD IMPERIAL CROWN (St. Edward's) is the one whose form is familiar from its frequent representations on the coin of the realm, the royal arms, etc. It was made for the Coronation of Charles II., to replace the one broken up and sold during the Civil Wars, which was said to have been worn by Edward the Confessor. With St. Edward's Crown, the act of Coronation is performed. It is of gold, and consists of two arches crossing at the top, and rising from a rim or circlet of gold, over a cap of crimson velvet, lined with white taffeta, and turned up with ermine. The base of the arches on each side is covered by a cross *pattée*; between the crosses are four *fleurs-de-lis* of gold, which rise out of the circle; the whole of these are splendidly enriched with pearls and precious stones. On the top, at the intersection of the arches, which are somewhat depressed, are a mound and cross of gold, the latter encircled with a fillet, the former richly jewelled, and adorned with three pearls, one on the top, and one pendent at each limb.

THE PRINCE OF WALES'S CROWN, so named, is of pure gold, unadorned by jewels. On occasions of State, it is placed before the seat occupied by the Heir Apparent to the Throne in the House of Lords.

THE QUEEN'S DIADEM, or circlet of gold, was made for the Coronation of Marie d'Este, consort of James II. It is richly adorned with large diamonds, curiously set, and the upper edge of the circlet is bordered with a string of pearls.

THE QUEEN CONSORT'S CROWN is the one used at Coronations when the sovereignty exists in the male branch, as on the present occasion. It is of gold, set with diamonds of great value

The Regalia of England

intermixed with pearls and other costly jewels. The cap is of purple velvet, faced with ermine. It is understood that considerable alterations will be made in the crown that will be used for Queen Alexandra's Coronation, enhancing both its worth and beauty. It is unnecessary to remind the Reader that no two crowns exactly fit the same head, and that a Queen Consort's crown is smaller in size—not merely officially, but actually—than a King's. Be that as it may, at all Coronations the crowns of King or Queen, with the possible exception of the old Imperial Crown (St. Edward's), is altered in size, and sometimes also in the general setting of the jewels by the Crown Jewellers; the suggested alterations being of course first of all submitted to the reigning sovereign for his sanction and approval.

*   *   *   *   *

THE IMPERIAL ORB, or MOUND (Fr. *monde*), is an emblem of sovereignty said to be derived from Imperial Rome; and to have been first adorned with the cross by Constantine, on his conversion to Christianity. It first appears among the royal insignia of England on the coins of Edward the Confessor; but, Strutt authenticates a picture, "made in the year 996," which represents that prince kneeling between two saints, who bear severally his sceptre and a globe, surmounted by a cross. This part of the regalia being indicative of supreme political power, has never been placed in the hands of any but Kings or Queens *Regnant.* In the anomalous case of William and Mary as joint sovereigns, another orb was made, and that spare orb (so to say) is still to be seen among the royal jewels of England. This orb is a ball of gold, 6 in. in diameter, encompassed with a band of gold, set with emeralds, rubies, and pearls. On the top is a remarkably fine amethyst, nearly $1\frac{1}{2}$ in. high, which serves as the foot or pedestal of a rich cross of gold, $3\frac{1}{4}$ in. high, encrusted with diamonds; having in the centre, on one side, a sapphire, and an emerald on the other; four large pearls at the angles of the cross, a large pearl at the end of each limb, and three at the base; the height of the orb and cross being 11 in.

THE QUEEN'S ORB is of smaller dimensions than the preceding, but of similar fashion and materials.

*   *   *   *   *

We now come to the Six Sceptres. First is

THE TEMPORAL SCEPTRE of gold, 2 ft. 9 in. in length; the staff very plain, but the pommel oramented with rubies, emeralds, and diamonds. The *fleurs-de-lis* with which this sceptre was originally adorned have been replaced by golden leaves, bearing the rose, shamrock, and thistle. The cross is variously jewelled, and has in the centre a large table diamond.

THE SPIRITUAL SCEPTRE, Rod of Equity, or Sceptre with the Dove, is also of gold, 3 ft. 7 in. long, set with diamonds and other precious stones. It is surmounted with an orb, banded with rose diamonds, bearing a cross, on which is the figure of a dove with expanded wings.

THE SCEPTRES, TEMPORAL and SPIRITUAL (William IV.), differ from the preceding, as shown in the illustration (Plate III.).

ST. EDWARD'S STAFF is a large golden rod 4 ft. $7\frac{1}{2}$ in. long, with pike of steel at the lower end, about $4\frac{1}{2}$ in. The staff has foliated ornaments, and a mound and cross at the top. It is carried before the Sovereign in the procession to the Coronation.

THE QUEEN'S IVORY SCEPTRE was made for Marie d'Este, consort of James II. It is mounted in gold, and terminated by a golden cross, bearing a dove of white onyx. This sceptre has been named, but without any historical authority, the sceptre of Queen Anne Boleyn.

THE AMPULLA is an antique vessel of pure gold, used for containing the holy oil at Coronations. It resembles an eagle with expanded wings, and is finely chased ; the head screws off at the middle of the neck, for pouring in the oil, and the neck being hollow to the beak, the latter serves as a spout, through which the consecrated oil is poured into—

THE ANOINTING SPOON, also of pure gold, has four pearls in the broadest part of the handle, and the bowl of the spoon is finely chased within and without. From its extreme thinness it appears to be sufficiently ancient ; but of what date, we know not.

THE SPURS (one of which is shown) are also used at Coronations. They are of gold, elaborately wrought at the edges and the fastening : they have no rowels, but end in an ornamented point, being what are commonly denominated prick spurs. New richly embroidered velvet straps were added to them for the Coronation of George IV.

THE ARMILLÆ, or BRACELETS, are of solid fine gold, chased, 1½ in. in breadth, edged with rows of pearls. They open by a hinge, and are enamelled with the rose, *fleur-de-lis*, and harp. Probably the *fleur-de-lis* will be altered for the thistle.

*　　*　　*　　*　　*

THE ROYAL SWORDS are named *Curtana*, or the Sword of Mercy, sheathed; the Sword of Justice to the Spirituality, which is obtuse; the Sword of Justice to the Temporality, which is sharp at the point; and the Sword of State. Of these, the last alone is actually used in the Coronation, being that with which the Sovereign is girded after the anointing; the rest are only borne in the procession by certain great officers of State.

A plain Gold Ring, with a large table ruby on which is engraved a plain or St. George's cross, is always prepared for the Coronation ; but, of course, it must be newly made, or, at least, set, for each sovereign.

*　　*　　*　　*　　*

In the same chamber with the Crowns, Sceptres, and other Regalia used in the sacred ceremonial of the Coronation, is a very interesting collection of Plate, formerly used at Coronation Festivals ; together with Fonts, etc. Among these are

THE BAPTISMAL FONT of silver, gilt, tastefully chased, and surmounted with two figures, emblematic

The Coronation of Edward VII

of the baptismal rite: this font was formerly used at the christening of the Royal Family; but a new font, of more picturesque design, was manufactured for her Majesty Queen Victoria.

THE SALT-CELLARS are worth the inspection of the curious, both for their singular forms and rich workmanship. The most noticeable is the Golden Salt-cellar of State, which is of pure gold, richly adorned with jewels, and grotesque figures in chased worked. Its form is castellated, and it has hence been called a "model of the White Tower," to which, however, it bears a very slight resemblance: the receptacles for the salt are formed by the removal of the tops of the turrets. There are, besides, in the Collection, two massive Coronation Tankards, of gold; a Banqueting Dish; and other dishes and spoons, of gold, used at Coronation Festivals; besides a beautifully wrought service of Sacramental Plate, employed at the Coronation, and formerly also used in the Chapel of St. Peter in the Tower.

It is interesting to read the following particulars, delivered by command to George the Fourth, drawn up by "the Master of the Jewels and the Commissioners of the Great Wardrobe," of such things as were

The Regalia of England

required to be delivered to the Bishop of Rochester, for the Coronation of King James the Second and Queen Mary. Those particulars run thus :—

FOR THE KING.

1. The Colobium Suidonis, a kind of surplice without sleeves, of fine linen or sarsenet.
2. The Supertunica, a close coat of cloth of gold, lined with crimson taffeta, and girt with a broad girdle and cloth of gold, to be put over the *Colobium.*
3. The Armilla, in fashion of a stole, of cloth of gold, to be put about the King's neck, and fastened above and beneath the elbows with silk ribbons.
4. A Pall of cloth of gold, in fashion of a cope.
5. A Pair of buskins, of cloth of gold.
6. A Pair of sandals, of cloth of gold.
7. A Shirt of fine Linen, to be opened in the places for the anointing.
8. Another Shirt of red sarsenet to be put over it.
9. A Surcoat of Crimson Satin, made with a collar for a band, both opened for the anointing, and closed with ribbons.
10. A Pair of under trousers and breeches to go

over them, with stockings fastened to the trousers, all of crimson silk.

11. A Pair of Gloves of linen.
12. A Linen Coif.
13. Three Swords: the *Curtana* or pointless sword called also the Sword of Mercy; the Sword of Justice to the Spirituality; and the Sword of Justice to the Temporality.
14. A Sword of State, with a scabbard richly embroidered.
15. Two Imperial Crowns set with jewels: one to crown the King; the other to be worn after his Coronation.
16. An Orb of gold, with a cross.
17. A Sceptre with a cross, called St. Edward's Sceptre.
18. A Sceptre with a Dove.
19. A Staff of gold with a cross at the top, and a pike at the foot, called St. Edward's Staff.
20. A Ring with a Ruby.
21. A Pair of gold Spurs.
22. An Ampul, or vessel of gold to hold the anointing oil, in shape of an eagle, and a spoon.
23. Two Ingots of gold, one weighing a pound,

and the other a mark, for the King's two offerings.

24. The Parliament Robes, viz., a Surcoat of Crimson velvet, with a hood furred with ermine and bordered with gold lace.

25. A Cap of State turned up with ermine.

26. The Robes of State of purple velvet of the same fashion as the former, and two caps of purple velvet turned up with ermine for the two crowns.

It is deserving of note, that those things mentioned and numbered consecutively 13 to 26, are still used in the Coronation of the Sovereign.

A second list headed, " Delivered to the Proper Officers for the Queen," runs thus :—

1. A Surcoat, or kirtle, of purple velvet, the sleeves turned-up and powdered with ermine.

2. A Robe, or Mantle, of purple velvet, with a long train, the cape and lining powdered with ermine, to wear over the surcoat.

3. A Circle, or Coronet of gold, to be worn before anointing.

4. A Crown with which she is to be crowned.

5. A smaller Crown to wear afterwards.

6. A Sceptre of gold with a cross.

The Coronation of Edward VII

7. An Ivory rod with a Dove.

8. A Ring.

It is to be noted that all these things (the first two somewhat altered in fashion) were used in the Coronation of Queen Charlotte, wife of George III., and also of Queen Adelaide, wife of William IV.

* * * * *

· The old Regalia were strictly Anglo-Saxon by their traditional names : The crown of Alfred, or of St. Edward, for the King ; the crown of Edith, wife of the Confessor, for the Queen. The sceptre with the dove is said to have been typical of King Edward's peaceful days after the expulsion of the Danes. The gloves were a reminder of his abolition of the Danegelt—a token that the King's hands should be moderate in taking taxes. The ring with which, as the Doge to the Adriatic, so the King to his people was wedded, was the ring of the pilgrim. The "great stone chalice" which was borne by the Chancellor to the altar and out of which the Abbot of Westminster administered the sacramental wine was believed to have been prized at a high sum "in Saint Edward's days." The form of oath retained till the time of James II. was to observe "the laws of the glorious Confessor." A copy

The Regalia of England

of the Gospels, purporting to have belonged to
Athelstane, was the book on which, as early as the

THE CORONATION, OR KING EDWARD'S, CHAIR.

fifteenth century, it was believed that the Coronation
oath was taken.

The ancient chair (of which we publish a sketch)
in which our Kings are crowned, known as "The

The Coronation of Edward VII

Coronation, or King Edward's, Chair," is considerably
over six hundred years old. It originally came
from Scone, in Scotland, whose Kings had also
been crowned in it. Edward the First of England
carried it away with him in 1297, from its ancient
repository in Scotland, and rendered it (along with
other of the old Scottish regalia, the golden sceptre
and crown among the number) as a solemn offering
at the shrine of Edward the Confessor. Ever
since then it has stood in the "Chapel of the
Kings" (the Confessor's Chapel) and been known
as St. Edward's Chair, being so designated in the
Coronation offices. In length, it is about 6 ft.
7 in. ; in breadth, at the seat, 38 in. ; in depth, 24 in. ;
and from the seat to the bottom, 25 in. Four
lions support each corner, leaving a space of 9 in.
between the chair and the bottom board, within
which space is enclosed a stone named "Jacob's
Stone" or the "Fatal Marble Stone" which King
Edward also brought out of Scotland, with the
ancient charter called "Ragman's Roll."

No end of legends' have grown up around the
Coronation Chair and the Stone of Scone, so called.
The origin of any stone being there at all, appears
to be traced to the primitive practice of raising

The Regalia of England

the kings of Gothic and Celtic race into an
elevated seat, generally of some natural stone, at
the time of their crowning. On the "Kings' stone,"
as we have elsewhere said, at Kingston-on-Thames,
the Anglo-Saxon sovereigns were crowned. And, in
Westminster Hall, dating back from a very early
period, the King, before he passed from the Palace
to the Abbey, was lifted to a marble seat, some
twelve feet long by three feet broad, standing at
the upper end of the Hall—probably where the
steps now lead to the House of Commons—then
known as "the King's Bench." Dean Stanley in
his "Memorials of Westminster Abbey" tells us
that "the Stone" of the Coronation Chair most
probably is the "stony pillow on which Columba
rested, and on which his dying head was laid in
his Abbey of Iona." "If so" (adds the Dean) "it
belongs to the minister of the first authentic
Coronation in Christendom"—the Coronation of
Aidan by Columba, A.D. 571. Edward I. brought
it out of Scotland from the Abbey of Scone. On
it he himself had been crowned King of the Scots.
We are told by the Dean, that in the last year of
Edward's reign the "venerable chair which still
encloses it was made for it by the order of its

captor; the fragment of the world-old Celtic races was embedded in the new Plantagenet oak." This is a grand old legend of an ancient and famous historical chair; and in so far as antiquarians have been able to collect and consider all the evidence, for, or against the truth of the legend, there is strong presumptive evidence that this, in fact, is none other than the famous Stone of Scone.

There is no doubt that in the Coronation Chair of Westminster Abbey, which so many of us have seen, every English sovereign has been crowned. Even Cromwell was installed in it, as Lord Protector, in Westminster Hall, whither it was carried from the Abbey for that singular and special occasion. When used at the Coronation it is cushioned, and richly covered with gold-beaten tissue, the better to disguise its time-stained and worm-eaten condition. There is also another coronation chair, similar in appearance to that described, save as to the four supporting lions, and enclosed stone, made for the use of Queen Mary II., when crowned with her consort, William of Orange. Needless to say that this second chair is also splendidly adorned, like the other, when brought into use for the crowning of the consort of the sovereign. We need not repeat the fable of " Jacob's stone." A legend goes that it was used as "a seat of justice" by some one living in the time of Moses! To accept of that statement, is to be endowed with a measure of credulity inconceivable in these days.

CROWNS OF THE KINGS OF ENGLAND

FROM THE TIMES OF THE ANGLO-
SAXON SOVEREIGNS TO THOSE
OF THE HOUSE OF STUART

When the Imperial Crown took the
Form as Illustrated in

THE REGALIA

Crowns of the Kings of England

EDGAR
(Cotton MS.)

EDGAR
(Cotton MS.).

EDWARD THE CONFESSOR
(Bayeux Tapestry).

EDWARD THE CONFESSOR
(Silver Coin, British Museum).

HAROLD II.

[FRANKISH].

[FRANKISH].

WILLIAM I.

187

The Coronation of Edward VII

WILLIAM I.

WILLIAM. I.

WILLIAM I.

WILLIAM II.

WILLIAM II.

HENRY I.

HENRY II.

RICHARD I.

Crowns of the Kings of England

JOHN.

HENRY III.

EDWARD I.

EDWARD II.

EDWARD III.

RICHARD II.

HENRY IV.

HENRY V.

HENRY VI.

HENRY VI.

EDWARD IV.

RICHARD III.

HENRY VII.

HENRY VIII.

EDWARD VI.

MARY.

Crowns of the Kings of England

JAMES I.

CORONATION MEDAL OF CHARLES I.

CORONATION MEDAL OF WILLIAM AND MARY.

CORONATION MEDAL OF QUEEN ANNE.

191

The Coronation of Edward VII

Among the Coronation paraphernalia, the State
Coach may be legitimately included, since it is not
only the most interesting of its kind in England,
but is said on good authority to be the most superb
state-carriage ever built. It was designed by Sir
William Chambers in 1761 for George III., and
cost in building something like £8,000. That king,
and his successors George IV., William IV., Queen
Victoria all used it for State purposes; King
Edward VII. at the opening of his first and second
Parliaments in 1901-2.

The paintings, which are by Cipriani, are very
rich. The front panel depicts Britannia seated on
a throne, holding in her hand a staff of Liberty,
attended by religion, justice, wisdom, valour, forti-
tude, commerce, plenty, and victory, presenting her
with a garland of laurel. In the background is a
view of St. Paul's and the River Thames. On the
right door Industry and Ingenuity, giving a cornu-
copia to the Genius of England, are presented,
while the panels on either side of the door depict
History recording the reports of Fame, and Peace
burning the implements of war. On the back panel
appear Neptune and Amphitrite issuing from their
palace in a triumphant car drawn by sea-horses,

Crowns of the Kings of England

attended by the winds, rivers, Tritons, Naïads, etc., bringing the tribute of the world to the British shore. The Royal Arms appear on the upper part of the back panel. They are beautifully ornamented with the Order of St. George, with the rose, shamrock, and thistle entwined. The left door shows Mars, Minerva, and Mercury, supporting the Imperial Crown of Great Britain, while the liberal arts and sciences protected are displayed on the panels on each side of the left door. The whole of the carriage and body is richly ornamented with laurel and carved work, beautifully gilded.

Weighing four tons, the coach is 24 ft. long by 8 ft. wide and 12 ft. high. The body is composed of eight palm trees, which, branching out at the top, sustain the roof; and four angular trees are loaded with trophies suggestive of the victories obtained by Great Britain. The trees are supported by four lions' heads. On the centre of the roof stand three cherubs, representing the Genii of England, Scotland, and Ireland, supporting the Imperial Crown of Great Britain, and holding in their hands the sceptre, sword of State, and ensigns of knighthood. The figures are adorned with festoons of laurel, which fall from thence towards the four corners.

Internally the Star, encircled by the Collar of the Order of the Garter, appears in the centre of the roof. Both are surmounted by the Imperial Crown, pendant, the George and Dragon. In the corners are the rose, shamrock, and thistle entwined. The hind lounge is ornamented with the badge of the Order of St. Michael and St. George, and on the front appears the badge of the Order of the Guelph and Bath, ornamented with rose, shamrock, and thistle. The hind seat fall has the badge of St. Andrew, and on the front the badge of St. Patrick.

The stately vehicle is richly gilded and entirely upholstered in crimson satin, with carpets, lace, and curtains to match. Crimson velvet covers the glass frames and the gun-metal shutter blinds. The hammercloth is gorgeous, and the supports are decorated with ornate carving.

It is not unlikely that an open coach, of more modern and convenient construction, which has been recently designed and built, may be used by the King and Queen on one of the days of the State Procession—possibly on both days. The design is most elaborate, and the cost of the carriage will be considerable. It is upholstered in rose-pink or crimson satin, like that used for the interior fittings of the State Coach.

The design for the Coronation medals is the work of the celebrated Austrian artist M. Fouch, who was summoned to Osborne to take a cast of Queen Victoria's features, prior to the removal of the remains to the *chapelle ardente*. On the obverse of the medal is a profile of the King and Queen, with an inscription around. On the reverse side is an elaborate and highly effective design, somewhat after the style adopted on the penny. Britannia is seated on a shield emblazoned with the Royal arms. Just above the shield is the date of the Coronation, June 26th, 1902. To the right of the figure of Britannia is a view of Westminster Abbey.

THE STATE COACH.

195

THE ROUTE

"ST. JAMES'S," querulously wrote Philip II. of Spain to Mendoza, one of the many ambassadors whose despatches he was so fond of correcting: "St. James's is a house of recreation which was once a monastery. There is a park between it and the palace, which is named Huytal; but, why it is named Huytal, I am sure I don't know." "Huytal" stands of course for Whitehall; and it was originally so called because of its whiteness or freshness of appearance, in comparison of the neighbouring York Place, in Tudor times the archiepiscopal residence in London of the Archbishops of York, among whom was Wolsey, the Cardinal.

The sumptuous palace that he erected on part of the site of old York Place, and which he occupied for some time during his chancellorship and prior to his downfall, was never, in fact, brought to completion. Had the Cardinal's palace as projected survived to the present, Whitehall

The Route

as now seen would probably have formed part of its buildings. Needless perhaps to remind the Reader that Wolsey's palace became the principal London residence of the sovereign, from Henry the Eighth's time to that of James the Second, when it was destroyed by fire. The palace and its appurtenances extended from near to what is now Northumberland Avenue, to Parliament Street, and from the riverside to St. James's Park. Wolsey, Henry VIII., Elizabeth, James I., Charles I., Cromwell, Charles II., and James II. all occupied it in turn. The only existing reminiscence of this historically famous, and once extensive and splendid range of buildings is the familiar Banqueting House, built by Inigo Jones, which originally served that purpose, then became a Chapel Royal, and so continued till a few years ago, when it became the museum of the Royal United Service Institution. The thoroughfare which extends from Charing Cross to Parliament Street is still called Whitehall, having been so known from the days of Wolsey.

Probably, no other thoroughfare in London has witnessed so many stirring scenes of state pageantry as this, or is so interwoven with the history of nearly every monarch who has occupied the English

The Coronation of Edward VII

throne. It formed part of the much frequented highway from the Tower to Westminster : first East Cheap, then Cheapside, then St. Paul's leading down to Ludgate, then the Temple and Temple Bar, then the Strand, Charing Cross, Whitehall, and Westminster. Just opposite the Banqueting House, on the site of the present Horse Guards, was the Tilt Yard, which in Elizabeth's time was the meeting-place of all sorts of gallant company. The Cockpit of the Stuarts was not far away, in the vicinity of what is now one of the oldest of London's streets, Downing Street, namely. The student of English history might people White-hall with the most famous men and women known to every period of that history, from the days of William the Norman to those of his present Majesty, Edward the Seventh ; for in all time it has been the high road to the King's ancient Palace of West-minster, whereof old Westminster Hall and the more modern Houses of Parliament are the present-day representatives ; the first dating back to 1397, the last-named to 1840. The King's Palace still survives, as we have before said, in the name of Palace Yard.

* * * * *

The Route

St. James's was never much of "a house of recreation" to the sovereigns of England unless, may be, to Henry the Eighth, when married to Anne Boleyn; and St. James's Palace was never a "monastery." It was originally a hospital for lepers, who were not in the condition of paupers. As a palace, judged by modern standards, it is but a poor example of such buildings, and its chief interest to-day centres in its age and history. It dates from Henry the Eighth, who "attached" it, like many another place he had set his mind on having. No part of the original St. James's Palace of Tudor days survives, except the familiar gateway facing St. James's Street, and the Chapel Royal. All the rest of the structure is comparatively modern, probably of no earlier date than the time of Queen Anne and the early Georges, if we except certain parts of the interior, preserved during the process of rebuilding, of which the chimney-piece in the Guard Chamber (if we remember aright) showing the initials of Henry the Eighth and Anne Boleyn may serve as an example.

Not the least interesting of the historic associations of St. James's Palace are connected with the Stuart kings. Although it is well known that Charles I.

took leave of his children, and passed his last night on earth in one of its rooms; it is not, perhaps, so generally known that the King's body was brought to St. James's Palace after the execution, was there embalmed and put in a coffin of lead, "and laid there a fortnight to be seen of the people." * From St. James's it was carried to Windsor, where it now rests in a vault in St. George's Chapel. Neither Cromwell nor the Parliament seem to have interfered with the King's friends in seeing to its decent interment, "provided that the expenses of the funeral did not exceed £500." It was even allowed to rest for a day in the King's chamber at Windsor Castle, whence it was carried to the Deanery and thence to the chapel.

Charles II. kept himself away from St. James's, not caring to be reminded of its mournful associations. His brother, James II., set up a society of Benedictine monks in the palace, and insisted on the consecration of the Papal Nuncio (Adda) as archbishop in the Chapel Royal. It was in the Queen's apartments, on the evening of the ceremony, that James, in presence of his court, fell on his knees before the newly consecrated prelate, and implored

* "England's Black Tribunal set forth," etc., 1658.

The Route

his blessing. " It was long indeed " (says Macaulay)
" since an English sovereign had knelt to mortal man ;
and those who saw this strange sight could not but
think of that day when John did homage for his
crown between the hands of Pandolph."

William of Orange came here the very night
that James finally fled from Whitehall. Here the
first Levée of the prince was held the following
day : "all the rooms and staircases were thronged ;
such was the press that men of the highest rank
were unable to elbow their way into the Presence
Chamber."

Queen Anne and the first three of the
Hanoverian kings used it as a palace, much more
than their predecessors ; and for many a long day
—for three centuries at least—functions of State,
Royal Proclamations, Royal Marriages, Christenings,
Balls, Banquets, Drawing-rooms, Levées, have taken
place at St. James's. During the reign of Queen
Victoria, one often read a state document dated " At
the Court at St. James's " ; and most of the Official
Announcements (1901) of King Edward the Seventh
are similarly dated : those, for example, publishing
the facts of his Accession and Proclamation as King.
His first Privy Council, where he announced that he

The Coronation of Edward VII

took the title of Edward the Seventh (as we have elsewhere noted), was held here.

The first Queen Mary died in St. James's Palace. Charles the Second was born here. General Monk took up his quarters here, while plotting the Restoration. Queen Anne considered it " quite the properest place to act such a cheat in " as that of the so-named "warming-pan" plot of James the Second's reign; the supposed conveyance of the child (afterwards known as the Old Pretender) to the Queen's bedchamber in that once familiar implement of domestic comfort.

The two German and English mistresses of George I. had apartments in the Palace ; as also had Mrs. Howard (afterwards Countess of Suffolk), mistress of George II. Here died Caroline, his queen ; and here also was born George IV. Queen Charlotte, wife of George III., rescued its memory from the many questionable associations belonging to it in the reigns of the King's two immediate predecessors. In George III.'s time, St. James's Palace became deadly dull, save for the Levées and Drawing-rooms periodically held in its state apartments. You may read all about the kind of life passed at St. James's in the concluding years of the eighteenth century in Madame D'Arblay's

The Route

memoirs. The odes of the Poets Laureate were, in bygone times, recited and sung before the king and queen in the Council Chamber. Several royal marriages, including those of George IV. and Queen Caroline and Queen Victoria and Prince Albert and some of their children, have been solemnised in the Chapel Royal, the oblong building situated between the Colour Court and Ambassadors' Court. The palace apartments are now chiefly occupied as offices or by personages of the King's Court. The Duke of Cornwall and York (now Prince of Wales) lived for a time in the only residence worthy of the name, that fronting on Cleveland Row.

So much, then, for St. James's, whose Tudor gateway is one of the oldest landmarks of London ; and whose park, street, square, and adjacent Pall Mall are among its most historic thoroughfares. The whole district is inseparably connected with the long history of the palace itself, and of those kings and queens who either lived there or at Whitehall, and in later years at Buckingham Palace. Marlborough House, from 1863 to 1901 the residence of King Edward the Seventh when Prince of Wales, fronts on the Mall. St. James's Street has been for centuries one of

The Coronation of Edward VII

the streets of London fashion and the centre of English club-life. St. James's Square, in the seventeenth century, was one of the lordliest places of residence of the Court quarter. Of Pall Mall, no more need be said than that probably no other street is so well known by name and reputation throughout the world. It is the Club-land of the empire.

* * * * *

When the Duke of Buckingham owned the house on the site of which Buckingham Palace now stands, an inscription in Latin ran thus over its main entrance: " Sic siti lætantur Lares "—the Household Gods delight in such a situation. That might have been the case in the days when George the First was King, and St. James's Park and all the land westward beyond open country. But times are changed and London has changed since those days. The domestic and familiar gods have long since departed from the place, whose garden was "a little wilderness full of blackbirds and nightingales," and whose mansion seems to have been one of the great attractions of London, no less architecturally than in location. This mansion came into possession of George III. by purchase in 1761, and fourteen years later was settled by Act of Parliament on

The Route

Queen Charlotte, and then became commonly known as "the Queen's House." Such are the few lines of history belonging to the King's principal residence in London, that named Buckingham Palace, fronting on St. James's Park, and in large part covering the ground once famous as the Mulberry Garden of the days of the Stuarts. It is more than probable indeed that the present north-west pleasure-grounds of the palace formed part of these very gardens, made so familiar to us in the writings of the dramatists of Charles II.'s reign.

No one could well mistake the ownership of Buckingham Palace, or the use to which it is appropriated. Its exterior indicates the state palace at a glance. It is an unsightly structure, adapted in part from old Buckingham House. Parliament was chary of money-voting for an entirely new palace in the reign of George the Fourth, having already found considerable sums for Carlton House and similar purposes, during the Regency and later reign of that king. The palace as we now see it was built in his day, and completed in the reign of his successor, William the Fourth, who, by the way, never lived in it, having freely expressed his dislike (so it is said) to the general appearance and discomfort of the whole structure. The late Queen (Victoria) entered upon occupation of the palace in June 1837 ; but when she was married considerable additions and alterations had to be made to it ; and it is probable that her Majesty least liked it of all the royal residences. In point of fact, it is less of a home than an official residence, set apart chiefly to purposes of state. For such purposes, its several apartments— Throne-room, Ball-room, Drawing-rooms, and Dining-room—are well adapted, being spacious, imposing, and splendidly furnished and decorated. It is now, however, the one Royal Palace of the Sovereign in London, used as a residence. St. James's is practically closed, except for occasional Levées in the Season ; and Kensington Palace has become a kind of national memorial of Queen Victoria (but let us not forget William the Third in this connection) ; just as Hampton Court has long been of the Tudor, Stuart, and early Hanoverian sovereigns. Kew is a mere cottage, interesting perhaps by reason of its associations with the last sad years in the life of George the Third.

*   *   *   *   *

The roadway leading from Buckingham Palace

The Route

to Hyde Park is named Constitution Hill. Whence
the name, and when actually bestowed, we are
unable to say. It used to be, and for aught we
know still is, a closed road for carriages, to all but
those of members of the Royal Family and privileged persons. Not so, however, to foot passengers ;
and it has always been a favourite spot with spectators of royal cavalcades, which almost invariably
proceed to and from Hyde Park, or to and from
Piccadilly, by this roadway. It was long known as
"the King's Coach-way to Kensington"—probably,
first so known in the days of William III., who
lived most of his time at Kensington Palace. Its
name was changed to Constitution Hill, so we are
inclined to think, when Queen Victoria first occupied
Buckingham Palace. The gates of the central archway at the northern, or Piccadilly, end are opened
only to carriages of the Royal Family.

* * * * *

Piccadilly begins at Apsley House exactly opposite
that archway—the town mansion for over thirty
years of the first Duke of Wellington, which contains
some fine historical and other pictures chiefly associated with the memory of the duke's career in the
Peninsula. Piccadilly is a fine open thoroughfare

for spectators on foot, and one also exceptionally well favoured in respect of opportunity of
sight-seeing from the windows of houses flanking
its north side. But, those are chiefly aristocratic
mansions or clubs, not available to the commonalty.
There are but two hotels along this section of the
Route ; and for accommodation at either we should
think prices would run high. The same remarks
hold good of St. James's Street, made up of clubs,
banks, insurance offices, and one or two well-to-do
tradesmen's shops, the upper portions of which are
commonly let out as gentlemen's "chambers." St.
James's Street's pavement, right and left, is free,
however, to the King's lieges, and, it need not be
said, to strangers not included within that category.

Pall Mall is, as every one knows, almost wholly
given over to clubs; the few exceptions being the War
Office on the south side, and a few shops and offices
on the north. If any of these last are available to
spectators, depend upon it that the prices demanded
would not be too moderate. All the way from
Waterloo Place to Trafalgar Square, Whitehall,
Parliament Street, and the precincts of the Abbey,
good vantage ground should be found. Those willing
to take their chance might find this district as

The Route

promising as any. In great London crowds, every one stands a chance of seeing what is going forward ; and many an indifferent or loitering spectator who comes upon the scene last, finds that he is as well placed as the majority who, maybe, have been in waiting for hours together. The great thing in a great London crowd is to keep oneself cool, and to obey the orders of the police. One remarkable characteristic of a great London crowd, in general, is its good temper and obedience to authority. The writer has been in many great London crowds in his time, and has sometimes found himself in more than "tight places" ; but he has never failed to find a way out by keeping cool, and showing a friendly confidence in his neighbours. Some of them may be pickpockets, or, more desirably, detectives. In either case, you will be much more likely to work out of a tight place, by keeping calm and showing yourself friendly—even if only for strategic reasons —than by any exhibition of "battery" or bad temper.

    *   *   *   *   *

All sorts of conjectures have been rife as to the Coronation Procession from the Palace to the Abbey. One has only to glance at the printed order of the service within the Abbey itself, to be assured

The Coronation of Edward VII

that Coronation Day must be very fatiguing to all concerned, from King and Queen to spectator. The length of the religious rite alone would be likely, one would say, to tire all but the most robust. A lengthy route of State Procession outdoors, to and from Westminster on that day, is hardly likely to be finally selected. We venture to think that one of three alternatives will be chosen in going or returning, as follows: either (1) by Constitution Hill to Piccadilly, St. James's Street, Pall Mall, Charing Cross, Whitehall; or (2) by way of Birdcage Walk and Great George Street; or (3) by the Mall of St. James's Park, through the Horse Guards, to Westminster.

It is generally understood, at the date of this book going to press, that there are to be two Coronation Processions through the streets of London: that, namely, on Friday, June 27th, the day following the ceremony itself, which second state-pageant is doubtless intended, shall take the place of the ancient time-honoured state procession from the Tower, through the City, to Westminster; and the principal, as above-stated, from the Palace to the Abbey on Coronation Day, Thursday, June 26th.

The Pageant of Friday, June 27th, will be so

The Route

arranged as to give the People in every part of
London, north and south of the Thames, ample
opportunity and space for seeing one of the most
splendid State Pageants that London has ever
witnessed. It is understood that his Majesty has
approved of the recommendation of the Executive
Coronation Committee, that the route, on the
occasion of the procession, should be the same as
that followed by the late Queen in 1897. It will
be generally recollected that on the occasion of the
"Diamond Jubilee" the Royal procession started
from Buckingham Palace shortly after eleven o'clock,
and proceeded by Constitution Hill, Piccadilly, St.
James's Street, Pall Mall, Trafalgar Square (north
side), Duncannon Street, Strand, Fleet Street, and
Ludgate Hill, to St. Paul's Cathedral. After the
ceremony the procession returned by the way of
the south side of St. Paul's Churchyard to Cheapside,
the Mansion House, King William Street, London
Bridge, Borough High Street, Borough Road, St.
George's Circus, Westminster Bridge Road, Westminster Bridge, Parliament Street, Whitehall, the
Horse Guards, and the Centre Mall to Buckingham
Palace.

It has been stated that one purpose of the lengthier

The Coronation of Edward VII

Procession is in some sort to revive the old-time associations of Westminster Hall with the King's Coronation. His Majesty, it is said, will make a call there to receive the addresses of various public bodies, and perhaps for the taking of oaths of allegiance. If this last incident should prove to be included in the day's proceedings, that would probably mean an abridgment of this part of the historic rite in the Abbey, more particularly referred to elsewhere in the printed religious services of the day.

*　　*　　*　　*　　*

We may take it that prices for seats to view the Procession will not rule higher than those asked on the day of Queen Victoria's Jubilee—that is to say, if the Route be not restricted solely to Constitution Hill, Piccadilly, St. James's Street, Charing Cross, Whitehall. Of course, the lesser the opportunity of seeing the Pageant, the higher will be the prices asked for accommodation. But, we should say—seeing we have had so many grand State processions of late years, and surely few could excel in splendour and interest that of June 1897 : we should say that a guinea or so should command a seat, from which conveniently to view either of the Coronation Processions of 1902.

The Route

"The Diamond Jubilee" of 1897 gave London a foretaste of what London can produce in the way of accommodation for the general public bent on sight-seeing. At the last Coronation in 1838 speculators were not perhaps so exacting or so numerous as on the occasion named; but there were a good many spacious timber structures— galleries they were called—built on the line of procession, seats in which commanded prices varying from 10s. to 30s. The front of Westminster Hospital, for example, was covered with a stand capable of holding some seven hundred persons, each of whom paid a guinea for a seat. The public stands extended all the way from Charing Cross down Whitehall to the Abbey. Even the equestrian statue of Charles I. was hemmed in by a wooden gallery. Prices for seats at the windows of houses on the line of route appear to have ranged from 10s. to £5 5s.; and the whole frontages of such houses were let for sums ranging from £50 to £300. In St. James's Street (then not so given over to clubs as now) several houses were let for £200. The old Reform Club-house was let to a speculator for £200, who realised £500 by his bargain.

THE PEOPLE

I F Pageantry be of any account in politics—and
he would be a bold, not to say ill-informed
citizen who should say to the contrary—it is of
service in striking the imagination of the multitude.
Otherwise, why a taste for flags and banners when
political elections come round? Why the stitching
by fair fingers of lovely silken rosettes of red, white,
blue and the like, and the display of such rosettes
on coats and gowns when the town is at fever heat
with patriotism—or "jingoism?" Why the hiring
of bands of music, banner-men, carriages, trumpeters,
and so on, and the arranging of processions, when
men take it into their heads to display their rejoicing,
that some particular section of the People are at
some particular juncture (say) in a worse position,
politically speaking, than themselves? Why, in
a word, State Processions through London's streets
at the King's Coronation, unless it be to show the
people that grandeur, splendour, soldiery, rank,
magnificence, the brilliance of coaches, the glitter of

The People

robes, jewels, uniforms, etc., etc., are part of the
paraphernalia of kings, offered in exchange, may
we not say, for the loyalty, goodwill, and support
of their people?

Even Demos himself, when the opportunity serves,
is not averse to appearing in public in state, so to
speak. He decorates with broad coloured sashes and
rich golden tassels, glistening stars of silver, medals,
aprons of white and blue, hats with plumes of
feathers, or other sightly and attractive insignia
peculiar to the guild, "mystery," brotherhood, or
other association to which perchance Demos and
his fellows to-day belong. Your thorough-paced
Radical, elected by the suffrages of his political
friends to County, Borough, or City councils, would
seem to consider that a scarlet or blue fur-trimmed
gown of broad-cloth, contributes not a little to the
dignity or imposing character of his office, or why
does he wear it? It would hardly be suggested, we
think, that every member of the Worshipful Court
of Aldermen of the City of London is an aristocrat?
No gentlemen are more ready to gratify the citizens
with a sight of gowns of scarlet, or "mazarine,"
of gold chains of office, maces, swords, cocked-
hats, plumes, uniforms, court dress, etc., than that

The Coronation of Edward VII

promiscuous gathering of gentlemen which to their own credit, no less than to the advantage and satisfaction of the City of London at large, carry on its municipal government.

Even the very Judges, the Clergy, and the Doctors are not averse to a little exhibition of display at times. The dignified judges of England, in full-bottomed wigs, scarlet robes, and ermine tippets, are quite as pleased to show themselves to the people, passing in procession to the opening of the High Courts of Justice in London, in Michaelmas Term, as the people are pleased to see them. As for the clergy who, from time immemorial, have been disposed to lecture their flocks—by the way, the last sermon preached by Bishop Latimer, before King Edward the Sixth, was in deprecation of finery; as for the clergy, who are always preaching against the pomps and vanities of this wicked world, among the which may be rightly included pomp and luxury of dress, some of themselves have been and still are among the greatest of sinners in these respects. The magnificence of Archbishop à Becket, we are told, was "incredible." Before the coming of Wolsey (so the chroniclers say) none wore silks and embroideries in England among the commonalty.

The People

The fact is, the most of us relish a little display, and all of us greatly relish a State display : all, perhaps, but those more immediately concerned in arranging and taking part in it.

The world sometimes thinks that kings and princes are very agreeably entertained, when they stand the central figures of the foremost group in some great function of State, surrounded by a splendid throng of statesmen, ambassadors, lords chamberlain, lords steward, masters of ceremonies, Crown equerries, gentlemen-at-arms and the rest, for the express purpose (in not a few instances) of gratifying a number of other people, whom they have never seen, and to whom the throne-room of the palace is not generally accessible. Many persons, I doubt not, view with envy the splendid positions that some of these great functionaries of a Court occupy, and doubtless would willingly forego their own independence to be allowed to stand for a time in their place. The great personages themselves, on the other hand, are only too delighted, we should imagine, to exchange the richly embroidered coat of scarlet and gold, or bullion and blue, for a plain everyday suit of honest " Cheviot " ; and, excepting for duty's sake, are no more entertained by the

The Coronation of Edward VII

proceedings of State processions, Foundation-stone layings, Levées, Drawing-rooms, State Balls, State Concerts, and the like, than a policeman is entertained by staring at the road traffic at Charing Cross.

I was curious to see what Charles Cavendish Fulke Greville (an aristocrat of the aristocrats, better known as sometime Clerk of the Privy Council and, later, author of the "Memoirs") might have to say about the Coronation of Queen Victoria, at which he, of course, was present. He gossips about it in a couple of pages, or so, and describes in a few words the scene in the Abbey. This is how he sums up his impressions : "The thing best worth seeing was the Town itself, and the countless multitudes through which the procession passed. . . . The great event of this Coronation is, that it was done for the people. To interest and amuse *them* [the word is printed in italics] seems to have been the principal object." And, as if to emphasise what was passing in his mind at the moment he wrote this, he mentions incidentally that the Chancellor of the Exchequer told him he had been informed, on good authority, that "£200,000 had been paid for seats alone." A Coronation is undoubtedly in a marked degree a serious, and imposing, historic and religious rite ;

218

The People

but the purely spectacular parts of the ceremony, the grand processions through London, the splendid scene in the Abbey, the attendant Court rejoicings and festivities : these are what mainly interest those who have not the good fortune to take any personal part in the ceremonial proceedings. Those who do happen to be appointed to take part in them find that "the thing best worth seeing is the Town itself."

Coronations were made for crowds. Apart from the national and political significance belonging to the act itself, and the interest inseparable from the solemn and imposing religious ritual connected with the ceremony, such great spectacles were planned and intended to interest and attract the People, and to arouse their loyalty and enthusiasm. It would be an original idea to give representatives of every rank of the King's subjects opportunity of witnessing the religious ceremonial, instead of reserving the whole space within the Abbey, as is usual, to the aristocratic and privileged few. On the eve of the Coronation, Westminster Abbey passes for the time into possession of the Crown and its officers ; so that there is not much chance, we fear, for "the great unknown" to mingle with

The Coronation of Edward VII

the well-known great, as spectators of the ceremony
itself.

*   *   *   *   *

Our old library friend, Pepys, who, in his time,
saw everything worth seeing in London, reports
that he was "up early" to witness the Coronation
of Charles the Second. "About four" (says he) "I
rose and got to the Abbey, and with much ado
did get up to a scaffold in the north end, where,
with a good deal of patience, I sat from past four till
eleven." That hour seems to have been the appointed
time for the religious ceremony of the Coronation
to begin, from time immemorial. Eleven is, as
every one knows, the Sunday morning church hour
common throughout England ; and as the Coronations of England's Sovereigns were generally
arranged to take place on some day appointed as
a Church Festival, it may be that that circumstance
had somewhat to do with the hour named. "At
daybreak" on that June morning sixty-four years
ago when Queen Victoria was crowned, the streets
of London were already thronged ; and grand folk,
an hour or two later, were making their way in
carriages to the Abbey. It might be as well to
note the fact here, for nearly all great State affairs

220

The People

are, as we have before pointed out, arranged and governed by ancient usage.

On Queen Victoria's Coronation Day, the special proceedings of the occasion were begun with a royal salute of twenty-one guns fired in St. James's Park at sunrise. The people began to form up in the streets and on the line of route as early as three in the morning. The doors of the Abbey were opened to those with tickets at 5 a.m. The House of Commons met shortly after 7 a.m., all members being in full-dress uniform or court dress, for the purpose of balloting for the places reserved to its representatives in the Abbey. At ten o'clock the Abbey doors were closed against all comers but those included in the procession of the Sovereign. It is most likely that the ceremony of the King's Coronation will be appointed for eleven or thereabout. Whether Londoners will throng the streets at "daybreak" on the day appointed is a point Londoners will decide for themselves. If they do not, it is probable that others will. Londoners have seen more of splendid State pageantry within the last ten or twelve years, than in all other years of her late Majesty's reign put together, unless we except the entry of Queen

The Coronation of Edward VII

Alexandra into London. For grandeur and interest alike, the Jubilee occasions would be hard to match ; but it is quite likely that the Coronation Processions to and from the Palace will at least equal those two memorable pageants in national interest. The King himself is partial to military display, which of all others appeals most to the popular interest. Why a naturally peace-loving people should be always so delighted with a sight of the pomp and circumstance of war—and the greater the military display the more satisfied and appreciative our non-combatant citizens are ; why the generally peace-loving citizen should most relish these warlike displays is a question we might leave to the consideration of philosophers.

*　　*　　*　　*　　*

Thackeray, in one of his earlier essays, incidentally mentions that he was in a "genteel crowd"—everything was "genteel" in Thackeray's time that was not positively vulgar : he was in a genteel crowd in one of the galleries of the Abbey at the Queen's Coronation. (We oldsters still cling to that dear old name, as if our late and long-time Sovereign Lady were yet with us.) Thackeray was in such a crowd, he said, "at the Queen's

The People

Coronation." In these times, we should probably write " a swell crowd." " In point of intelligence," he proceeds to remark, " the democrats were quite equal to the aristocrats "—a comparison, shall we say, not quite in the style of Thackeray of the days of " Esmond." " I have never yet been in an English mob," he continues, " without the same feeling of respect for the persons who composed it, and without wonder at the vigorous and orderly good sense, and intelligence, of the People." When we remember that Thackeray was somewhat less familiar with the People than his great contemporary Dickens, such an admission from him is worth repeating. When we speak of " the People," some of us are apt at times to fancy that we ourselves are not of their number. The author of " Vanity Fair," who mostly moved in the upper circles of society, loved his club, and the well-arranged households and inviting companionship of the well-to-do, somewhat condescendingly as it seems to us, uses the word " mob " to express his view of a great popular gathering in the streets of London. Grammatically speaking, no doubt, " mob " is sufficiently correct. But we usually employ that word now to signify the rowdier element

The Coronation of Edward VII

in popular assemblies. Now, if there be one feature of our English crowds more than another that astonishes the stranger, not less than the Englishman himself, it is the remarkable absence of rowdyism. "The vigorous and orderly good sense, and intelligence," and wholesome respect for the authority of the police, which in general characterises a great London crowd, or "mob" if you will, may be classed among the most astonishing and pleasing features of our times.

We venture to say that not the least interesting of the many interesting sights to be seen in London on the day of the King's Coronation, will be the People gathered in numbers overwhelming in its streets; hundreds of thousands of the People, of every class, drawn from near and far, as orderly, good-tempered, and law-abiding as any to be seen in any city in the world. That sight, to be seen, most probably, in the Park fronting on the Palace, on Constitution Hill, in Piccadilly, in St. James's Street, in Pall Mall, at Charing Cross, about Whitehall, at Westminster, and elsewhere, will be one of the great features of the day of the crowning of King Edward at Westminster. The crowd will be in the main attracted, of course, by a desire to

224

The People

see the State pageantry of the Royal Procession itself to and from the Abbey; but it will also be drawn together from all parts of the kingdom, . to show its good-will, and proclaim its loyalty, to the reigning monarch, son and successor of Queen Victoria the Well-beloved, who passed this way to her Coronation, amid the same scenes of popular rejoicing, now so many years ago.

ARRANGEMENT, ACCORDING TO PRECEDENT, OF THE ALTAR AND THE
"THEATRE" (SO-NAMED) IN WESTMINSTER ABBEY AT THE
CORONATION.

THE ABBEY

H E who is without enthusiasm, if any there be, for this that has been not unfitly named " the most lovely and lovable thing in Christendom "; he who may be as yet unversed in the history and traditions of London's famous Minster of the West, would do well to turn for a moment to the " Memorials of Westminster Abbey " by the late Dean Stanley, for a little pleasant and profitable reading, preparatory to that event of which the Abbey, as heretofore, is the central point of greatest interest.

He says that " the most continuous succession of events " the Abbey has witnessed in its eight centuries of history have been the coronations. No similar succession of events is recorded of any other building in the world. The crowning of the old-time kings of France at Rheims and of

The Coronation of Edward VII

the Popes of Rome in the Basilica of the Vatican most nearly approaches to it. But Rheims is now deserted, and the present Church of St. Peter at Rome is, by five hundred years, more modern than Westminster Abbey. Moreover, no other coronation rite in Europe reaches back to so early a period, as that of the sovereigns of Britain. The crowning of Aidan by Columba is the oldest known ceremony of the kind in Christendom ; and, from the Anglo-Saxon "order" of the coronation of Egbert is derived the ancient form of the coronation of the Kings of France. Only in two European countries, besides Britain, does the rite retain its full primitive signification, in Hungary, namely, and in Russia.

* * * * *

The traditionary place of the first crowning of a British sovereign is far-famed Stonehenge by Salisbury Plain. Of the Anglo-Saxon kings of England, seven were crowned on "the King's Stone"—so says tradition—"by the first ford of the Thames" Londonwards travelling from the west. The stone itself (so at least is commonly supposed) still stands an interesting memorial in the market-square at Kingston-on-Thames, that

The Abbey

picturesque suburb of London, not too curiously sought nowadays by strangers and pilgrims, but which is within a pleasant walk of town by way of Putney and Wimbledon Common, thence through Kingston Vale. Winchester Cathedral and St. Paul's in London—the elder church once standing on the site of the present metropolitan cathedral—were likewise coronation places of the Saxon kings of England. It appears still to be doubtful where Harold of that line was crowned. But, with his successor (as we have already pointed out) began that long series of successive coronations in the Abbey of Westminster, of which that of King Edward the Seventh, and his Queen, will be for some years to come (as we trust) the present appropriate finale.

Founded in the eleventh century of our era by his famous ancestor, alike in lineage, and in name, it is peculiarly befitting and not less interesting that Edward the Seventh should, in the second year of the twentieth century, receive the homage of the nation, and be crowned king in the Church of St. Peter " of our Palace at Westminster,"—for so his present Majesty's Proclamation of June 26th, 1901, ran—like all his ancestors of the name. The

The Coronation of Edward VII

third of the Henrys kings of England prided himself on his descent from King Alfred. Henry's sons were the first of the English princes who were called by Anglo-Saxon names. That king's first-born son—the first prince, be it said, ever born at Westminster—received his name from the Anglo-Saxon founder of the Abbey—"the first of that long series of Edwards, which is the one royal name that constantly reappears, to assert its unchanging hold on the affections of the English people."

Plainly and briefly stated, the Ceremony of the Coronation of the King at Westminster is the recognition, and confirmation, in Solemn Form of his royal descent, and consequent right of Accession to the throne. The ceremony itself is not absolutely necessary, though held essential, for the security of the title to the Crown. William the Fourth, "the Sailor King" of England, was eager to dispense with it altogether. In theory, and according to ancient law of the Realm (as every one knows) the King never dies. The Queen is dead, live the King! The throne is never vacant. At 6.30 p.m. on the evening of January 22nd, 1901, at Osborne, Albert Edward, the eldest son of the greatly loved and deeply

The Abbey

lamented Queen Victoria, became King in fact and in person. The Coronation "at Our Palace at Westminster" is the solemn public confirmation of King Edward's right.

The ceremonial itself is more splendid, elaborate, and emblematic in England, than in any other country of Europe. Its ritual is in the highest degree interesting, being so faithfully established upon, and regulated by, historic precedent. The practice of anointing with oil, for example, has been continued for upwards of a thousand years in Britain at the Coronation of the Sovereign. Some of the forms still in use would appear to be of Judaical origin, at all events in the religious part of the ceremonies. It was declared by Thomas à Becket, Archbishop of Canterbury, that "kings are anointed on the head to signify their glory; on the breast to signify their sanctity; and on the arm to declare their power." These various acts of consecration, so many centuries old, are still done by the Archbishop of Canterbury at the Coronation in Westminster Abbey. The various insignia, hereinbefore referred to, such as a ring to signify faithfulness, the bracelet for good works, a sceptre for justice, a sword for vengeance, the purple robes

The Coronation of Edward VII

to attract reverence, the diadem to blazon glory, are all of much historic interest. The word "king" (as the text-books say) signifies power, or knowledge, "wherewith every sovereign should be endowed." His formal crowning, apart from the illustrious honour and dignity thus conferred, tends to a formal establishment of those rights which the People claim from a monarch, in return for the duty and allegiance the People are bound to render him.

There was a book in the keeping of the Abbots of Westminster, one of the most interesting of the treasures still in custody of the Deans, named the "Liber Regalis," or "Book of the Royal Offices." Its date is of the middle years of the fourteenth century. That book has furnished the precedents

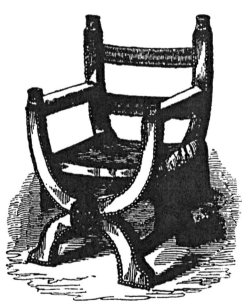

CORONATION CHAIR OF QUEEN MARY TUDOR.

The Abbey

for the religious ceremonies of the Coronations in Westminster Abbey ever since. Queen Mary was crowned according to the order therein set forth. Queen Elizabeth's coronation followed the same order in most respects. King James the First's took what is known as "the new form," which, "with some alterations, has been 'the Coronation Service' in use down to the present day." The service used in 1838, at the coronation of Queen Victoria, was "edited," if we may so say—prepared, perhaps, would be a better word— by Archbishop Howley, then of Canterbury, and Primate of All England, who presided at the ceremony. It is undoubtedly based on, or collated with, that used at the crowning of James the Second and Queen Mary, which was also the precedent followed at the crowning of King George III. and Queen Charlotte, George IV., and King William IV.

*   *   *   *   *

From the time of William the Conqueror, the Archbishop of Canterbury has (with three exceptions) always been the chief ecclesiastic at the Coronations; and the Bishop of London has usually preached the sermon. The Archbishop of York

The Coronation of Edward VII

is appointed to assist. Dean Stanley says that, "on these occasions only, these three prelates take their places, as of right, in the Choir of the Abbey, but the Archbishop of York has been obliged to remain content with the inferior and accidental office of crowning the Queen Consort, as was originally performed by Aldred (Archbishop of York) for Queen Matilda, two years after the Conqueror's coronation." By 1 William and Mary, c. 61, it is enacted "that the Coronation may be performed by the Archbishop of Canterbury, or the Archbishop of York, or either of them, òr any other Bishop whom the King's Majesty shall appoint." The claim of the Archbishop of Canterbury to preside at the marriage of royal personages (it may be mentioned) rests on the theory that the kings and queens of England are "parishioners" of the see of Canterbury.

Parenthetically: to illustrate the close connection that has always existed between the Crown and Westminster Abbey, it may be mentioned that the Coronations even to this day—it was so in times remote, when Tudor and Stuart came to the throne, and is so now when Edward the Seventh is to be crowned—are said to take place at "Our Palace at

The Abbey

Westminster," whereof the Houses of Parliament may be said to be the present-day representatives. They are still referred to as the Palace of Westminster, and the open space in front of the Hall is still known as Palace Yard, held to be within the precincts (we believe) of the House of Commons. At all events, this space is practically closed to the public when Parliament is in session.

*　　*　　*　　*　　*

On that eventful Christmas Day of the year 1066, when William the Norman passed to his crowning at Westminster, the suburbs of the city, the streets of London—such as they then were—and all the approaches to the Abbey were thronged with a vast crowd. So say the historians. Double rows of soldiers, horse and foot, kept it in hand. That king's was a coronation, the like of which (save in Richard the First's case) has not been seen in England from those days to these. William was left almost alone at the altar, with none but Archbishop Aldred, and his terrified priests, to take the coronation oath of the Anglo-Saxon kings, to which, by the way, he added a solemn promise of his own, to treat his new-found subjects as well as the best of their kings had done. There was

The Coronation of Edward VII

a tumult, and almost a fight, brought about by a
misconception of the meaning of the shouts of
"Yea! Yea!" and the uplifting of swords within
the Abbey, when the assembled Normans and
English were asked, in the language of each,
whether they would have William for their king.

The coronation of Richard the First (the Lion
Hearted), who took the crown from the altar with
his own hands, "in signification that he held it
only from God," and delivered it to the Archbishop,
who then placed it on the king's head; Richard's
coronation, done in such swift and unceremonious
fashion, ended in a wholesale butchering and
plundering of the Jews—though utterly against the
king's will, as old Speed would have us believe.
When Queen Mary was crowned, "a relic of the
true cross" was exposed on the altar. That relic,
spirited away when her successor came to the
throne, turned up in an old box, containing some
antique ecclesiastical vestments, some two centuries
later, and tradition says was long-time kept in the
Benedictine College of St. Gregory near Bath.

Pennant cynically remarks, "an abbey is nothing
without relics"; and he proceeds to enumerate
some of those in the centuries long past belonging

The Abbey

to Westminster Abbey. For example, "the veil and some of the milk of the Virgin Mary, the blade-bone of St. Benedict, the fingers of St. Alphage, the head of St. Maxilla, and half the jaw-bone of St. Anastasia." What became of these sacred treasures of the ancient abbey of pre-Reformation times? It is strange nowadays to think, that for at least five centuries the service of the Roman Catholic Church was daily performed in St. Peter's in Westminster, and that many of our kings and queens were crowned there by the archbishops of that Church and according to its rites. John Feckenham of Queen Mary's reign, when "the old religion" was revived for a while, was (if we remember aright) the last Abbot of Westminster who presided at a coronation.

The first detailed account of the ceremonial of the Coronation as continued to our time dates from Richard I. (1189): namely, the procession from the Palace to the Abbey; the emblematic swords, the sceptre, the spurs, the fact of the Bishops of Durham, and Bath and Wells (then first named in this capacity) supporting the King on the right hand and left; the oath; the anointing; the crown, taken by the King himself in this instance from the

The Coronation of Edward VII

RICHARD THE SECOND IN HIS CORONATION ROBES (FROM THE PORTRAIT IN WESTMINSTER ABBEY).

altar, and given to the Archbishop. At the succeeding coronation of John (1199), a peculiar function was added. The barons of the Cinque Ports were, for services rendered the King by sea, appointed to carry the state canopy over his Majesty as he passed to the Abbey, and also at the ceremony of anointing.

As regards incidental matters of the ceremony, it may be mentioned that the "Knights of the Bath" are first mentioned in the procession of Edward III.; the "King's Champion" (now an obsolete functionary) also appeared for the first time then; the "Yeomen of the Guard" fell into position first of all at Henry VII.'s coronation; the Peers of Parliament in their robes, the Knights of the Garter in the dress of their order, the great officers of state in gorgeous uniform, the heralds in crimson and gold, appear to have been first seen in all their magnificent setting of to-day, at the coronation in Westminster Abbey of Queen

The Abbey

Anne Boleyn, on Sunday, June 1st, 1533; the King himself of his own design being absent from that ceremony.

The prayer—"Almighty God, of His Mercy, let the light of His countenance shine upon your Majesty, grant you a prosperous and happy reign, defend, and save you; and let your subjects say Amen—'God save the King!'"—formed the peroration of Archbishop Cranmer's sermon in the Abbey at the Coronation of the Boy-King Edward VI. It seems that to Cromwell was first handed the Bible—"a Book of Books which doth contain both precepts and examples for good government"—when he was installed Lord Protector. Cromwell was not crowned and anointed in Westminster Abbey, but was solemnly enthroned, girt with a sword of state, clad in a robe of purple, and presented with the Bible, in Westminster Hall. The period of the Commonwealth marks the one break in the continuity of eight centuries, when· he who for the time was king in all but name and right of royal succession, was not invested with the attributes of royalty, the crown, the sceptre, and the orb, in Westminster Abbey. It is interesting at this distance of time to note how Cromwell himself respected the ancient traditions of the Abbey as the place of coronation of the English Kings ; and was content himself to be enthroned and invested with the robe of purple in the adjoining Hall. But, if we are to credit history, Cromwell was at one time seriously contemplating the step which would have led him to the more sacred historic edifice only a few yards away ; probably some time before that day when the Crown jewels of the realm were seized in the Abbey treasury by order of the Parliament, and broken up.

When Cromwell had in turn vanquished and destroyed King, Lords, and Commons, and seemed (as the historian says), "to be left sole heir of the powers of all three," it was within the bounds of possibility that he might "mount the ancient English throne, and reign according to the ancient English polity." According to Macaulay, Cromwell was not without thoughts of settling the affairs of the sorely tried kingdom in some such fashion. "The peers who now remained sullenly at their country houses, and refused to take part in public affairs, would, when summoned to their house by the writ of a king in possession, gladly resume their ancient functions. Northumberland

The Abbey

and Bedford, Manchester and Pembroke, would be proud to bear the crown, and the spurs, the sceptre, and the globe before the restorer of aristocracy." Such things, however, were not to be. " The title of king was not revived, but the kingly prerogatives were entrusted to a Lord High Protector. The sovereign was called not his Majesty, but his Highness."

James the Second ordered Sancroft to abridge the coronation ritual. The reason given out to the public was that the day—April 23rd (St. George's Day), 1685—was too short for all that was to be done. The real reason was to forego that part of the ritual likely to be offensive to the religious feelings of Roman Catholics. The Communion Service was left out. The ceremony of presenting the Bible was omitted. But the King showed no scruples as to making the customary oblation on the altar. " He appeared to join in the petitions of the Litany chanted by the Bishops. He received from those false prophets the Unction typical of a divine influence ; and knelt with the semblance of devotion while they called down upon him the Holy Spirit of which they were in his estimation the malignant and obdurate foes. Such are the inconsistencies of human nature that this man who, from a fanatical zeal for his religion, threw away three kingdoms, yet chose to commit what was little short of an act of apostasy rather than forego the childish pleasure of being invested with the gewgaws symbolical of kingly power." So writes Macaulay.

George the Third appears to have studied the ritual of the coronation beforehand, and knew more about it than those officials of his court who should have known most. There is a funny story told of the answer made by the Deputy Earl Marshal of that day (the Earl of Effingham) to some complaint of the King, as to certain omissions made in the ceremony: "It is true, Sir," said the Earl, "there has been some neglect; but I have taken care that the next coronation shall be regulated in the exactest manner possible." If the Deputy Earl Marshal had it no longer in his power to make good the promise when the next coronation came, George the Fourth himself saw to it that no omissions were made in any part of the ceremony when he was crowned. This anecdote reminds us of another of a similar kind, in regard of things which had been better left

The Abbey

unsaid. George the Second happened to be chatting with the beautiful Lady Coventry of his day on the topic of court pageants. The only sight, the lady told him, she was now eager to see, was a coronation! The old King laughed heartily and repeated the story in high good humour at the supper-table. A few months ago we saw this same story published in a London newspaper, and attributed to a beautiful American lady conversing with the Prince of Wales during Queen Victoria's lifetime. Of such ancient stories is the gossip of contemporary history made up.

Those interested in omens may perchance know the story told of one of the finest jewels in the state crown of George the Third becoming loosened, and falling to the ground at the coronation banquet in Westminster Hall. Jesse relates the anecdote, and further says that many remembered the event when later the American colonies were lost to England. A similar story is told of James the Second. The crown, not fitting well, tottered on the King's head in the Abbey, and was only prevented from falling off by Henry, the brother of the patriot Algernon Sidney, who happened to be near the King. " It is not the first time, Sir,"

The Coronation of Edward VII

he said, "that a member of our family has supported the crown." Yet a third story is told, of Charles the First's walking-stick falling to the floor at his trial in Westminister Hall, and of the gold head becoming detached. This story is repeated by many relaters of the events of that time, who also add that the King was greatly disturbed at the omen, as well he might have been. It is not impossible that each of these anecdotes may be traced to ancient writers of fiction. We merely repeat them for what they are worth.

* * * * *

Not the least interesting of the treasures belonging to the Abbey are the ancient copes, worn (as some may remember) by the officiating clergy at the Jubilee of 1887. Some of the existing copes, purple, crimson, and cloth of gold, were originally made, we believe, for the Coronation of Charles II., though there is one of curious design, which is said to have been brought from Spain for the Coronation of Queen Victoria. Time, however, has wrought sad havoc here, for several of these once-splendid vestments have lost their colour, and are no longer suitable for wear. The crimson copes are to figure

The Abbey

once more at the Coronation, with others of the same Royal colour and no less magnificent.

The choirs of the Abbey and the Chapel Royal, St. James's, will form the backbone of the musical performers. For many years a prominent position at the Coronation has been assigned to these two historic bodies. They will probably be largely reinforced—indeed, it is possible that efforts will be made to secure the presence of representatives from every cathedral choir in the land. In addition to the time-honoured Coronation anthems of Handel and Attwood, some musical novelties (such is commonly the case) may be expected which have never before been heard in such a service.

There were rumours in London towards the close of 1901 that the Coronation Office was to be curtailed. In the belief that this was in contemplation the Church newspapers of various grades of opinion, began to protest vigorously against the possible omission of the celebration of the Holy Communion and the anointing of the Sovereign. We should not have mentioned this incident, except for the fact that it gave occasion for a leading article in one of the newspapers referred to, which doubtless presented the view of the

The Coronation of Edward VII

"High Church" party, respecting certain parts of
the religious rite.

In that article the writer observed of the ceremony :

> "If it is anything more than a mere pageant, a
> piece of silly theatrical display, comparable to the
> Lord Mayor's Show, it is the solemn consecration of
> the King's person for his great office. It is strictly
> analogous to the ordination of a priest, the sacring
> of a Bishop, and the order of service is constructed
> on the same lines. The King's sacring takes place
> in the course of the celebration of the Divine Liturgy,
> and, as in all similar cases, the person consecrated
> partakes of the Holy Communion. Only once in the
> long list of English coronations has this rule been
> broken. It was in the case of James II., who refused
> to communicate with the Church of England. He
> consented, with little consistency, to be crowned,
> anointed, and blessed by the Archbishop of Canter-
> bury, but he insisted on leaving the Abbey without
> communicating. The omission of the anointing (if
> that indeed be contemplated) is even worse. We
> confess that we cannot imagine why the King should
> go to Westminster at all, if not for the unction. To
> suppose this a mere ceremony, accidentally attached
> to the Coronation service, is to miss the whole mean-
> ing of the rite. It is not too much to say that the
> anointing is the one distinctively sacred act by which
> the King is set apart for his holy office. . . . The

246

The Abbey

crowning, and the investment of the King with mantle, sceptre, sword, and the other regalia, however solemn and significant a ceremony, has nothing of an essentially sacred character. It might be done with equal propriety, if with less solemnity, in Westminster Hall or in the House of Lords. It might be done by any high officer of State." *

* * * * *

When one is bidden to a splendid and imposing ceremonial, the most splendid and imposing, indeed, of any that he can expect to witness in London in a lifetime; it is not to be supposed that he is in the humour for paying much heed to reflections on the vanity of things in general. Otherwise, we might be tempted to offer the following— if the Reader be not already familiar with

CORONATION MEDAL OF MARY TUDOR.

* *The Church Times*, November 22nd, 1901.

247

The Coronation of Edward VII

them—for consideration. They are quite as likely to provide nourishing food for thought within the Abbey while patiently waiting for the hour of eleven to boom forth from Big Ben, as the day's gossip provided by the London journals. We quote from the one-time largely read Jeremy Taylor : " A man may read a sermon " (wrote he), " the best and most passionate that ever man preached, if he shall but enter into the Sepulchre of Kings. In the same Escurial where the Spanish princes live in greatness and power, and decree war or peace, they have wisely placed a cemetery where their ashes and their glory shall sleep till time shall be no more. And where our Kings have been crowned their ancestors lie interred, and they must walk over their grandsire's head to take his crown. There is an acre sown with royal seed, the copy of the greatest change—from rich to naked, from ceiled roof to arched coffins, from living like gods to dying like men. There is enough to cool the flames of lust ; to abate the height of pride ; to appease the itch of covetous desires ; to sully and dash out the dissembling colours of a lustful, artificial, and imaginary beauty. There the warlike and the peaceful, the fortunate and the miserable, the beloved and the

The Abbey

despised princes mingle their dust, and pay down
their symbol of mortality ; and tell all the world,
that when we die, our ashes shall be equal to kings,
and our accounts easier, and our pains, or our
crowns, shall be less."

      *   *   *   *   *

THE PROCESSION

AS regards the interior arrangements of the Abbey for the Coronation service, from the great West door, at which the Procession enters, to the screen which divides Choir from Nave, two rows of galleries have heretofore been erected; on each side, that is to say, of the centre aisle—the one gallery level with the vaultings, the other with the summit of the western door. These galleries, the backs of which would rest against the wall of the Abbey, have their fronts fluted with crimson cloth, richly draped at the top, and decorated with broad golden fringe at the bottom. The seats in these galleries were supposed to provide accommodation for some fifteen hundred persons. It is somewhat doubtful, however, if galleries so lofty will be raised now.

On the floor of the centre aisle a slightly raised platform, or carpeted way, is laid down, along which the King's and Queen's Procession passes to the

The Procession

Choir. This is matted over, and covered with crimson cloth. On the pavement of the aisle itself bordering this carpeted way, stand the military told off to keep the line of the Procession clear.

The " Theatre " (p. 226), where the principal parts of the opening ceremony are enacted, lies immediately under the central tower of the Abbey, and is in fact a square, formed by the intersection of the choir and transepts, extending nearly the whole breadth of the choir. On this square a platform is erected, ascended by five steps. The summit of this platform, and also the highest step leading to it, is covered with richest cloth of gold. From that step, down to the flooring of the " Theatre," all is covered with carpet of rich red or purple colour, bordered with gold. In the centre of this " Theatre," the sumptuously draped chair is placed for the Sovereign, in which he receives the homage of the peers ; and a little aside from it another for the Queen Consort. At the north-east end of this " Theatre " a pulpit is erected from which the Coronation sermon is preached.

In the sacrarium, which forms part of the altar-

The Coronation of Edward VII

space, the Coronation chairs stand—the ancient chair known as King Edward's, and that of later date know as Queen Mary's. It is here the King and Queen are crowned.

Right of the altar, looking towards it, accommodation is provided for members of the Royal Family; and on the left a bench is provided for the Bishops, while above them in a kind of low gallery or "box" are ranged the Foreign Ambassadors and special envoys. The back of the altar itself is draped with purple and gold silks; and the floor of the sacrarium is covered with a rich purple and gold carpet. Above the altar in time past were the galleries reserved to the members of the House of Commons; but this arrangement is hardly likely to be made now.

In the Choir itself, all the ordinary stalls, reading-desks, and pews are removed. In their places are erected, on each side of the Choir, five rows of benches, covered with scarlet drapery and gold, reserved as seats for the great officers of State and Household. To the peers and peeresses are usually allotted galleries in the transepts, north and south. There they sit in all the glittering pomp of velvet and ermine.

Baptismal
Font

State
Salt Cellar

The Procession

According to ancient usage, the Procession from the West door of the Abbey to the Choir was thus marshalled:

The Prebendaries of Westminster.
The Very Reverend the Dean.
Pursuivants.
Heralds.

Equerries-in-Waiting Gentleman Ushers Grooms-in-Waiting
on the King. to the King. on the King.

The Comptroller of his Majesty's Household.

The Treasurer of his Majesty's Household [bearing the crimson bag with the Coronation Medals], attended by two gentlemen.

Sergeants-at-Arms.

Sergeants-at-Arms.

Private Secretary to the King.
The Vice-Chamberlain, acting for the Lord Chamberlain of his Majesty's Household, attended by an officer of the Crown Jewels Office, bearing on a cushion the Ruby Ring and Sword of the King.
The Lord Privy Seal.

The Keeper of the Privy Purse.
The Lord Steward of his Majesty's Household.

The Lord President of the Council.

The Lord Chancellor of Ireland, attended by his Purse-bearer.
The Lord Archbishop of Armagh.
The Lord Archbishop of York.
The Lord High Chancellor, attended by his Purse-bearer.
The Lord Archbishop of Canterbury.
The Princesses of the Blood Royal in their Robes of State, each attended by a Lady and Gentleman of their Household.
THE REGALIA OF THE SOVEREIGN.

St. Edward's Staff, borne by a Peer.
The Golden Spurs, borne by a Peer.
The Sceptre with the Cross, borne by a Peer.

253

The Coronation of Edward VII

The Third Sword, borne by a Peer.	Curtana, or Sword of Mercy, borne by a Peer.	The Second Sword, borne by a Peer.
Gentleman Usher of the Black Rod.	The Queen Consort's Regalia.	Garter Principal King at Arms.

The Lord Great Chamberlain of England.

The Princes of the Blood Royal in their Robes of State, each attended by two Gentlemen of their Household.

The High Constable of Ireland.		The High Constable of Scotland.
The Earl Marshal of England.	The Sword of State, borne by a Peer.	The Lord High Constable of England.
The Sceptre with the Dove, borne by a Peer.	St. Edward's Crown, borne by the Lord High Steward.	The Orb, borne by a Peer.
The Patina, borne by a Bishop.	The Bible, borne by a Bishop.	The Chalice, borne by a Bishop.

THE KING'S MOST EXCELLENT MAJESTY,
in his
Royal Robe
or Mantle of
Crimson Velvet
furred with Ermine
and bordered with
Gold Lace,
accompanied by
her Majesty
THE QUEEN CONSORT,
in her Royal Robes
of Purple Velvet
turned up with Ermine,
and wearing a circlet of gold
adorned with jewels.
The trains in each case
borne by Ladies and Gentlemen
of the Royal Household.
Gentlemen-in-Waiting on the King.
Ladies-in-Waiting on the Queen.
The Lord Chamberlain.

(left margin) The Gentlemen-at-Arms with their Standard Bearer.

The Bishop of Bath and Wells.

The Bishop of Durham.

(right margin) The Honourable Corps of Gentlemen-at-Arms with their Lieutenant.

The Procession

*　　*　　*　　*　　*

Let us once again as serviceable reminder when
the occasion comes, glance back at precedent for
the exact times on the last Coronation Day (Queen
Victoria's), when such or such a thing was appointed to take place according to the official
programme published. We have already (p. 221)
referred to some of the details.

First of all, then, the Day itself was inaugurated
with the firing of a royal salute at sunrise—a
quarter before 4 a.m. Soon after that hour, the
privileged spectators, people with tickets for stands,
and windows, on the line of route of the Procession
began to move to their places. The Abbey doors
were opened at 5 a.m. to all comers with tickets;
but many of the best seats were found to have
been already occupied as early as 3 a.m. By ·
6 o'clock the arrivals had become very frequent;

255

The Coronation of Edward VII

and at 7 a.m. the Earl Marshal's officers found
more than they could do, to usher peers and
peeresses to their places. The House of Commons
began to assemble at 7 o'clock—"some dressed in
full court dress, many in naval and military uniforms
with orders, and a large number wearing the
Windsor uniform." The Speaker took the chair
at nine o'clock ; and " all the members rose to receive
him." Prayers having been read, the Speaker
informed the House that, " in order to secure
perfect fairness in the allotment of the seats in
the Abbey, reserved to members of the House of
Commons, the counties would be balloted for ;
and requested that the members for each County,
and each Borough within the county, should on
the name of the County being called, leave the
House and proceed to the Abbey." About ten o'clock,
Mr. Speaker himself, preceded by the Mace, his
chaplain, and by the clerks at the table, passed
across to the Abbey.

At 10 a.m., the doors of the Abbey were closed
against all persons but the Sovereign and suite,
the Ministers of State, official attendants, and the
Foreign Ambassadors. At that hour, the great
officers of State, appointed to carry the Regalia,

The Procession

along with the Archbishops of Canterbury and York, and the Bishops of Bangor, Lincoln, and Winchester, assembled in the Jerusalem Chamber to receive the different articles which they had to carry at the ceremony. In that chamber, the Regalia had been deposited over-night in custody of the Dean of Westminster. They were now delivered by him to the Lord Chamberlain of the Household, who delivered them to the Lord High Constable, who gave them to the Lord Great Chamberlain, who handed them over to the several noblemen and bishops appointed to receive them :

1. St. Edward's Staff.
2. The Spurs.
3. The Sceptre with the Cross.
4. The Pointed Sword of Temporal Justice.
5. The Pointed Sword of Spiritual Justice.
6. Curtana, or Sword of Mercy.
7. The Sword of State.
8. The Sceptre with the Dove.
9. The Orb.
10. St. Edward's Crown.
11. The Patina.
12. The Chalice.
13. The Bible.

Proceeding at ten o'clock, the Sovereign's Pro-

The Coronation of Edward VII

cession began to move from Buckingham Palace. At 11 the solemn and sacred ceremony in the Abbey was begun. At half-past precisely, a salvo of artillery (forty-one guns) announced to the people that the chief act, the actual ceremony of the Crowning of the Sovereign, had then been done. At 3.30, the Coronation ceremony was concluded, so that it actually occupied first to last, in the Abbey, four hours.

Eleven thousand tickets in all were issued for seats within Westminster Abbey, a considerable number of which were allotted to privileged personages—peers, peeresses, M.P.'s, public officials, officers of the army and navy, foreign representatives, etc., etc.

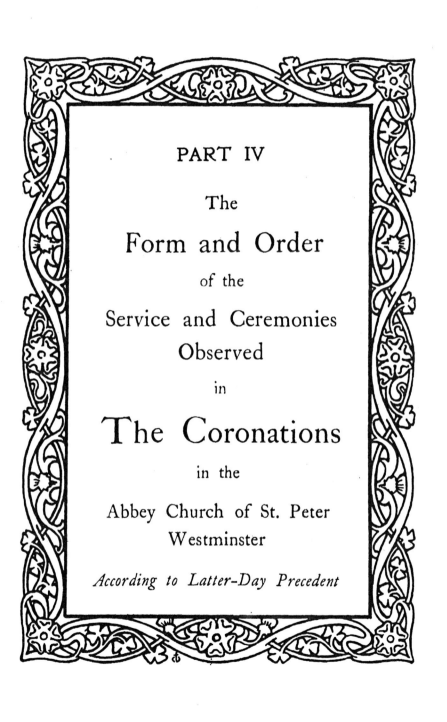

PART IV

The

Form and Order

of the

Service and Ceremonies
Observed

in

The Coronations

in the

Abbey Church of St. Peter
Westminster

According to Latter-Day Precedent

THE CONTENTS OF THIS PART

The Contents of this Part

THE FORM & ORDER OF THE CORONATION SERVICE

THE particulars hereinafter following, which are at this moment of historic and general interest alike, are taken from a copy of the official edition of "The Form and Order of the Coronation Service," published by the Queen's Printers in 1838. With some slight necessary variation in the wording of the Prayers, that Form and Order is almost certain to be followed on the present occasion. At all events, the ancient and historic ritual will, in every probability, be closely kept to.

All such matters in England are based on the ancient precedents which have from immemorial time, in the matter at present under review, followed the order of the "Liber Regalis" of Westminster Abbey, incidentally referred to on p. 232. The Reader will notice what we have said on p. 233 touching the precedents followed at Queen Victoria's coronation. In respect of the crowning of the Queen Consort, the order of James II. and Mary says: "The Queen was then anointed, crowned, invested, and enthroned with the same ceremonies"—that is, as the King. Up to that Section, the service will doubtless be so arranged as to include both their Majesties King Edward and Queen Alexandra. We have ventured to make only such slight alterations in the published copy as would necessarily be made. The Queen Consort's rite will probably follow the order of George III. and Queen Charlotte, which (as we have said) followed that of King James II. and Queen Mary.

Form and Order of the Service

IN the Morning upon the Day of the Coronation early, Care is to be taken that the *Ampulla* be filled with Oil, and, together with the *Spoon*, be laid ready upon the Altar in the Abbey Church.

SECT. I.

The Entrance into the Church.

The King and Queen, as soon as They enter at the West Door of the Church, are to be received with the following Anthem, to be sung by the Choir.

ANTHEM.

I WAS glad when they said unto me, We will go into the House of the Lord. For there is the Seat of Judgment, even the Seat of the House of David. O pray for the peace of Jerusalem, They shall prosper that love Thee. Peace be within thy walls, and Prosperity within thy Palaces.

Glory be to the Father, &c.

The King and the Queen in the mean time pass up through the Body of the Church, into, and through the Choir, and so up the Stairs to the Theatre*; and having passed by the Throne, they make Their humble Adoration, and then kneeling at the Faldstools set for Their Majesties before Their Chairs, use some short private Prayers; and, after

* A raised stage or platform erected between the choir and the sanctuary, of which we publish a sketch, p. 226.

Form and Order of the Service

sitting down (not in the Throne, but in Their respective Chairs before, and below, the Throne), there repose Themselves.

SECT. II.

The Recognition.

The King and the Queen being so placed, the Archbishop turneth to the East part of the Theatre, and after, together with the Lord Chancellor, Lord Great Chamberlain, Lord High Constable and Earl Marshal (Garter King of Arms preceding them), goes to the other three sides of the Theatre in this Order, South, West, and North, and at every of the four sides, with a loud Voice, speaks to the People : And the King in the mean time standing up by His Chair, turns and shews Himself unto the People at every of the four sides of the Theatre, as the Archbishop is at every of them, and while He speaks thus to the People :

SIRS, I here present unto you King EDWARD, the Undoubted King of this Realm : Wherefore all you who are come this Day to do your Homage, Are you willing to do the same ?

The People signify their Willingness and Joy, by loud and repeated Acclamations, all with one Voice crying out,

God save King EDWARD.

Then the Trumpets sound.

SECT. III.

[*But see Note preceding (p. 263), as to the crowning of the Queen Consort.*]

The First Oblation.

The Bible, Paten, and Cup being brought by the Bishops who had borne them, and placed upon the Altar, the Archbishop goeth to the Altar and puts on his Cope, and standeth on the North Side of it : And the Bishops, who are to read the

The Coronation of Edward VII

Litany, do also vest themselves. And the Officers of the Wardrobe, &c. spread Carpets and Cushions on the Floor and Steps of the Altar.

Which being done, the King, supported by the two Bishops, of *Durham*, and *Bath* and *Wells*, and attended by the Dean of *Westminster*, the Great Officers and the Lords that carry the *Regalia* going before Him, goes down to the Altar, and kneeling upon the Steps of it makes His *First Oblation* ; Which is a *Pall*, or *Altar-Cloth* of *Gold*, delivered by an Officer of the Wardrobe to the Lord Great Chamberlain, and by Him, kneeling, to His Majesty : and an Ingot or Wedge of Gold of a pound weight, which the Treasurer of the Household delivers to the Lord Great Chamberlain, and He to His Majesty, kneeling : Who delivers them to the Archbishop, and the Archbishop standing (in which posture he is to receive all other Oblations) receives from Him, one after another, the Pall to be reverently laid upon the Altar, and the Gold to be received into the Bason, and with the like Reverence put upon the Altar.

Then the Archbishop saith this Prayer, the King still kneeling :

O GOD, who dwellest in the high and holy Place, with them also who are of an humble Spirit, Look down mercifully upon this Thy Servant EDWARD our King, here humbling himself before Thee at Thy Footstool, and graciously receive these Oblations, which in humble Acknowledgment of Thy Sovereignty over all, and of Thy great Bounty to Him in particular, He hath now offered up unto Thee, through Jesus Christ our only Mediator and Advocate. *Amen.*

The King having thus offered, and so fulfilled his Commandment, who said, *Thou shalt not appear before the Lord thy God empty*, goes to His Chair set for Him on the South side of the Altar, where He is to kneel at His Faldstool when the Litany begins.

Form and Order of the Service

In the mean time, the Lords who carry the *Regalia*, except those who carry the Sword, come in Order near to the Altar, and present Every One what He carries to the Archbishop, who delivers them to the Dean of *Westminster*, to be by Him placed upon the Altar, and then retire to the Places and Seats appointed for Them.

SECT. IV.

The Litany.

Then followeth the Litany, to be read by two Bishops, vested in Copes, and kneeling at a Faldstool above the Steps of the Theatre, on the middle of the East side thereof, the Choir reading the Responses.

O GOD the Father of heaven : have mercy upon us miserable sinners, &c.

[After the Prayer, "We humbly beseech Thee," &c., followeth,]

O GOD, who providest for thy people by thy power, and rulest over them in love, grant unto this thy servant our KING the spirit of wisdom and government that being devoted unto thee with all His heart, He may so wisely govern this kingdom, that in His time thy Church and People may continue in safety and prosperity ; and that persevering in good works unto the end He may through thy mercy come to thine everlasting kingdom, through Jesus Christ Thy Son Our Lord. *Amen.*

THE Grace, &c.

The Bishops who read the Litany will resume their Seats.

The Coronation of Edward VII

The beginning of the Communion Service.

Sanctus.

Holy! Holy! Holy, Lord God of Hosts;
Heaven and Earth are full of thy Glory;
Glory be to Thee, O Lord most High;

Amen.

Then the Archbishop beginneth the Communion Service.

OUR Father, &c.

Collect.

ALMIGHTY God, unto whom all hearts be open, &c.

¶ Then shall the Archbishop, turning to the People, rehearse distinctly all the Ten Commandments ; and the People, still kneeling, shall after every Commandment ask God Mercy for their transgression thereof for the time past, and Grace to keep the same for the time to come, as followeth.

Archbishop.

GOD spake these words, and said, &c.

¶ Then shall follow this Collect for the King, the Archbishop standing as before, and saying,

Let us pray.

ALMIGHTY God, whose kingdom is everlasting, &c.

The Epistle,
To be read by one of the Bishops.

1 Pet. ii. 13.

268

HENRY THE SEVENTH'S CHAPEL.

269

The Coronation of Edward VII

The Gospel,

To be read by another Bishop, the King with the People standing.

S. Matt. xxii. 15.

Then the Archbishop readeth the *Nicene* Creed; the King with the People standing, as before.

I BELIEVE in one God, &c.

The Service being concluded, the Bishops who assisted will return to their seats.

SECT. VI.

The Sermon.

At the end of the Creed one of the Bishops is ready in the Pulpit, placed against the Pillar at the North-East Corner of the Theatre, and begins the Sermon, which is to be suitable to the great Occasion; which the King and Queen hear sitting in their Chairs on the South side of the Altar, over against the Pulpit.

On the King's right hand stands the Bishop of *Durham*, and beyond him, on the same side, the Lords that carry the Swords: On His left hand the Bishop of *Bath* and *Wells*, and the Lord Great Chamberlain.

On the North side of the Altar sits the Archbishop in a purple Velvet Chair; Near the Archbishop stands Garter King of Arms: on the South side, East of the King's Chair, nearer to the Altar, stand the Dean and Prebendaries of *Westminster*.

SECT. VII.

The Oath.

The Sermon being ended, and His Majesty having on Thursday the 14th day of February, 1901, in the presence of the Two Houses of Parliament, made and signed the

Form and Order of the Service

Declaration, the Archbishop goeth to the King, and standing before Him, says to the King,

Sir, Is your Majesty willing to take the Oath?

And the King answering,

I am willing.

The Archbishop ministereth these Questions; and the King, having a Copy of the printed Form and Order of the Coronation Service in his Hands, answers each Question severally, as follows.

Archb. Will You solemnly promise and swear to govern the People of this United Kingdom of *Great Britain* and *Ireland*, and the Dominions thereto belonging, according to the Statutes in Parliament agreed on, and the respective Laws and Customs of the same?

King. I solemnly promise so to do.

Archb. Will You to Your Power cause Law and Justice, in Mercy, to be executed in all Your Judgments?

King. I will.

Archb. Will You to the utmost of Your Power maintain the Laws of God, the true Profession of the Gospel, and the Protestant Reformed Religion established by Law? And will You maintain and preserve inviolably the Settlement of the Church of *England* and of *Ireland*, and the Doctrine, Worship, Discipline, and Government thereof, as by Law established within *England* and *Ireland*, and the Territories thereunto belonging? And will you preserve unto the Bishops and Clergy of *England* and *Ireland*, and to the Churches there committed to their Charge, all such Rights and Privileges, as by Law do, or shall appertain to Them, or any of Them?

King. All this I promise to do.

The Coronation of Edward VII

Then the King arising out of his Chair, attended by His Supporters, and assisted by the Lord Great Chamberlain, the Sword of State being carried before Him, shall go to the Altar, and there make His Solemn Oath in the sight of all the People, to observe the Promises: Laying His right hand upon the Holy Gospel in the Great Bible, which was before carried in the Procession, and is now brought from the Altar by the Archbishop, and tendered to Him as He kneels upon the Steps, saying these Words:

The things which I have here before promised, I will perform and keep.   So help me God.

A Silver Standish to be brought. Then the King kisseth the Book, and signeth the *Oath.*

SECT. VIII.

The Anointing.

The King having thus taken His Oath, returns again to His Chair on the South Side of the Altar; and kneeling at his Faldstool, the Archbishop beginneth the Hymn, *Veni Creator Spiritus*, and the Choir singeth it out.

HYMN.

COME, Holy Ghost, our souls inspire,
  And warm them with thy Heav'nly fire.
      &c., &c., &c.

This being ended, the Archbishop saith this Prayer:

O LORD, Holy Father, who by anointing with Oil didst of old make and consecrate Kings, Priests, and Prophets, to teach and govern thy People Israel: Bless and Sanctify thy Chosen Servant EDWARD, who by our Office and Ministry is now to be anointed with this Oil, and consecrated King of this Realm: Strengthen Him, O Lord, with the Holy Ghost the Comforter; Confirm and Stablish Him with thy free and Princely

Form and Order of the Service

Spirit, the Spirit of Wisdom and Government, the Spirit of Counsel and Ghostly Strength, the Spirit of Knowledge and true Godliness, and fill Him, O Lord, with the Spirit of thy Holy Fear, now and for ever. *Amen.*

This Prayer being ended, the Choir sing :

ANTHEM. 1 Kings i. 39, 40.

ZADOK the Priest, and Nathan the Prophet, anointed Solomon King; and all the People rejoiced and said; God save the King, Long live the King, May the King live for ever. Amen. Hallelujah.

At the Commencement of the Anthem, the King rising from His Devotions, goes before the Altar, attended by His Supporters, and assisted by the Lord Great Chamberlain, the Sword of State being carried before Him, where His Majesty is disrobed of His Crimson Robes.

The King will then sit down in *King Edward's* Chair placed in the midst of the *Area* over against the Altar, with a Faldstool before it, wherein He is to be anointed. Four Knights of the Garter hold over Him a rich Pall of Silk, or Cloth of Gold; the Anthem being concluded, the Dean of *Westminster* taking the *Ampulla* and *Spoon* from off the Altar, holdeth them ready, pouring some of the Holy Oil into the Spoon, and with it the Archbishop anointeth the King, in the Form of a Cross,

On the Crown of the Head, and on the Palms of both the Hands, saying,

Be Thou anointed with Holy Oil,* as Kings, Priests, and Prophets were anointed :

* At the Coronation of James II., "this Oil was by the King's order, prepared by James Amond, Esq., Apothecary to the King and Queen, . . . and was solemnly consecrated on the morning of the Coronation by the Dean of Westminster, assisted by the Prebendaries." Sandford, p. 91, Note.

273

The Coronation of Edward VII

And as Solomon was anointed King by Zadok the Priest, and Nathan the Prophet, so be You anointed, blessed, and consecrated King over this People, whom the Lord your God hath given you to rule and govern, In the Name of the Father, and of the Son, and of the Holy Ghost. *Amen.*

Then the Dean of *Westminster* layeth the *Ampulla* and *Spoon* upon the Altar, and the King kneeleth down at the Faldstool, and the Archbishop standing on the North side of the Altar, saith this Prayer or Blessing over Him :

OUR Lord Jesus Christ, the Son of God, who by his Father was anointed with the Oil of gladness above his fellows, by his Holy Anointing pour down upon your Head and Heart the Blessing of the Holy Ghost, and prosper the Works of your Hands : that by the Assistance of his Heavenly Grace you may preserve the People committed to your charge in Wealth, Peace, and Godliness ; and after a long and glorious Course of ruling this Temporal Kingdom Wisely, Justly, and Religiously, you may at last be made Partaker of an Eternal Kingdom, through the Merits of Jesus Christ our Lord. *Amen.*

This Prayer being ended, the King arises, and sits down again in His Chair.

SECT. IX.

The presenting of the Spurs and Sword, and the Oblation of the said Sword.

The *Spurs* are brought from the Altar by the Dean of *Westminster*, and delivered to the Lord Great Chamberlain, who, kneeling down, presents them to the King, who forthwith sends them back to the Altar.

BRONZE GATE, HENRY THE SEVENTH'S CHAPEL.

275

The Coronation of Edward VII

Then the Lord, who carries the *Sword of State*, returns the said Sword to the Lord Chamberlain (who gives it to an Officer of the Jewel House, to be deposited in the Traverse in *King Edward's* Chapel) and receiveth in lieu thereof, from the Lord Chamberlain, another *Sword*, in a *Scabbard* of *Purple Velvet*, which he will deliver to the Archbishop, who, laying it on the Altar, saith the following Prayer:

HEAR our Prayers, O Lord, we beseech Thee, and so direct and support thy Servant King EDWARD, that He may not bear the Sword in vain; but may use it as the Minister of God for the terror and punishment of Evil-doers, and for the protection and encouragement of those that do well, through Jesus Christ our Lord. *Amen.*

Then the Archbishop takes the *Sword* from off the Altar, and (the Archbishops of *York* and *Armagh*, and the Bishops of *London* and *Winchester*, and other Bishops, assisting, and going along with him) delivers it into the King's Right Hand, and He holding it, the Archbishop saith:

RECEIVE this Kingly Sword, brought now from the Altar of God, and delivered to You by the hands of us the Bishops and Servants of God, though Unworthy. With this Sword do Justice, stop the Growth of Iniquity, protect the holy Church of God, help and defend Widows and Orphans, restore the things that are gone to decay, maintain the things that are restored, punish and reform what is amiss, and confirm what is in good Order: that doing these things, You may be glorious in all virtue: and so faithfully serve our Lord Jesus Christ in this Life, that You may reign for ever with him in the Life which is to come. *Amen.*

Then the King, rising up, and going to the Altar, offers the Sword there in the Scabbard, delivering it to the Arch-

Form and Order of the Service

bishop, who places it on the Altar ; the King then returns and sits down in *King Edward's* Chair : And the Lord who first received the Sword offereth the Price of it, and having thus redeemed it, receiveth it from off the Altar, by the Dean of *Westminster*, and draweth it out of the Scabbard, and carries it naked before His Majesty during the rest of the Solemnity.

The Archbishops and Bishops who had assisted during this Oblation will return to their Places.

SECT. X.

The Investing with the *Royal Robe,* and the Delivery of the *Orb.*

Then the King arising, the *Imperial Mantle*, or *Dalmatic Robe*, of Cloth of Gold, lined or furred with Ermine, is by an Officer of the Wardrobe delivered to the Dean of *Westminster*, and by him put upon the King, standing : The King having received it, sits down, and then the *Orb* with the Cross is brought from the Altar by the Dean of *Westminster*, and delivered into the King's Right Hand by the Archbishop, pronouncing this Blessing and Exhortation :

RECEIVE this Imperial Robe, and Orb, and the Lord Your God endue You with Knowledge and Wisdom, with Majesty and with Power from on High ; The Lord clothe You with the Robe of Righteousness, and with the Garments of Salvation. And when You see this Orb set under the Cross, remember that the whole World is subject to the Power and Empire of Christ our Redeemer. For He is the Prince of the Kings of the Earth ; King of Kings, and Lord of Lords : So that no man can reign happily, who derives not his

The Coronation of Edward VII

Authority from him, and directs not all his Actions according to His Laws.

The King delivers His Orb to the Dean of *Westminster*, to be by Him laid on the Altar.

SECT. XI.

The Investiture *per Annulum & Baculum.*

Then an Officer of the Jewel House delivers to the Lord Chamberlain the King's *Ring*, who delivers the same to the Archbishop, in which a Table Jewel is enchased ; the Archbishop puts it on the Fourth Finger of His Majesty's Right Hand, and saith :

R ECEIVE this Ring, the Ensign of Kingly Dignity, and of Defence of the Catholic Faith ; and as You are this day solemnly invested in the Government of this earthly Kingdom, so may You be sealed with that Spirit of Promise, which is the Earnest of an heavenly Inheritance, and reign with Him who is the blessed and only Potentate, to whom be Glory for ever and ever. *Amen.*

Then the Dean of *Westminster* brings the *Sceptre* and *Rod* to the Archbishop ; and the Lord of the Manour of *Worksop* (who claims to hold an Estate by the Service of presenting to the King a Right Hand Glove on the Day of His Coronation, and supporting the King's Right Arm whilst He holds the Sceptre with the Cross) delivers to the King a Pair of *rich Gloves*, and upon any Occasion happening afterwards, supports His Majesty's Right Arm, or holds His Sceptre by Him.

The Gloves being put on, the Archbishop delivers the Sceptre, with the Cross, into the King's Right Hand, saying,

R ECEIVE the Royal Sceptre, the Ensign of Kingly Power and Justice.

278

Form and Order of the Service

And then he delivers the Rod, with the Dove, into the King's Left Hand, and saith,

RECEIVE the Rod of Equity and Mercy: and God, from whom all holy desires, all good counsels, and all just works do proceed, direct and assist You in the Administration and Exercise of all those Powers which he hath given You. Be so merciful, that You be not too remiss; so execute Justice, that You forget not Mercy. Judge with Righteousness, and reprove with Equity, and accept no Man's Person. Abase the Proud, and lift up the Lowly; punish the Wicked, protect and cherish the Just, and lead your People in the way wherein they should go: thus in all things following His great and holy example, of whom the prophet *David* said, " Thou "lovest Righteousness, and hatest Iniquity; The Sceptre "of Thy Kingdom is a right Sceptre;" even Jesus Christ our Lord. *Amen.*

SECT XII.

The putting on of the Crown.

K. *Edward's* Crown.—The Archbishop, standing before the Altar, taketh the Crown into his Hands, and laying it again before him upon the Altar, saith,

O God, who crownest thy faithful Servants with Mercy and loving Kindness; Look down upon this thy Servant EDWARD our King, who now in lowly Devotion boweth His Head to thy Divine Majesty; and as thou dost this day set a Crown of pure Gold upon His Head, so enrich His Royal Heart with thy heavenly Grace; and crown Him with all Princely Virtues, which may adorn the high Station wherein thou hast placed Him, through Jesus Christ our Lord, to whom be Honour and Glory for ever and ever. *Amen.*

The Coronation of Edward VII

Then the King still sitting in King *Edward's* Chair, the Archbishop, assisted with the same Archbishops and Bishops as before, comes from the Altar ; the Dean of *Westminster* brings the Crown, and the Archbishop taking it of him, reverently putteth it upon the King's Head. At the sight whereof the People, with loud and repeated Shouts, cry, *God save the King*, and the *Trumpets* sound, and by a Signal given, the great Guns at the *Tower* are shot off. As soon as the King is crowned, the Peers, &c., put on their Coronets and Caps.

The Acclamation ceasing, the Archbishop goes on, and saith,

BE strong and of a good courage ; Observe the Commandments of God, and walk in His Holy ways : Fight the good Fight of Faith, and lay hold on Eternal life ; that in this World You may be crowned with Success and Honour, and when You have finished your Course, receive a Crown of Righteousness, which God the Righteous Judge shall give You in that Day. *Amen.*

Then the Choir singeth this Anthem :

ANTHEM.

THE King shall rejoice in Thy strength, O Lord : exceeding glad shall He be of Thy Salvation. Thou hast presented Him with the Blessings of Goodness, and hast set a Crown of pure Gold upon His Head. Hallelujah. *Amen.*

SECT. XIII.

The presenting of the Holy Bible.*

Then shall the Dean of *Westminster* take the *Holy Bible*, which was carried in the Procession, from off the Altar, and deliver

* This ceremony was first introduced at the Coronation of William and Mary, in 1689. But, see the reference to Cromwell in Chapter " The Abbey."

Form and Order of the Service

it to the Archbishop, who with the same Archbishops and Bishops as before going along with him, shall present it to the King, first saying these Words to Him :

OUR Gracious King; we present You with this *Book*, the most valuable thing that this world affords. Here is Wisdom ; This is the Royal Law ; These are the lively Oracles of God. Blessed is he that readeth, and they that hear the Words of this Book ; that keep, and do, the things contained in it. For these are the Words of Eternal Life, able to make you wise and happy in this world, nay wise unto salvation, and so happy for evermore, through Faith which is in Christ Jesus ; to whom be Glory for ever. *Amen.*

Then the King delivers back the Bible to the Archbishop, who gives it to the Dean of *Westminster*, to be reverently placed again upon the Holy Altar, the Archbishops and Bishops who had assisted returning to their Seats.

SECT. XIV.
The Benediction, and *Te Deum.*

And now the King having been thus anointed and crowned, and having received all the Ensigns of Royalty, the Archbishop solemnly blesseth Him : And all the Bishops, with the rest of the Peers, follow every part of the Benediction, with a loud and hearty *Amen.*

THE Lord bless and keep you : The Lord make the light of his Countenance to shine for ever upon you, and be gracious unto you : The Lord protect you in all your ways, preserve you from every evil thing, and prosper you in every thing good. *Amen.*

The Lord give you a faithful Senate, wise and upright Counsellors and Magistrates, a loyal Nobility, and a dutiful Gentry ; a pious and learned and useful Clergy ; an honest, industrious, and obedient Commonalty. *Amen.*

The Coronation of Edward VII

In your days may Mercy and Truth meet together, and Righteousness and Peace kiss each other; May Wisdom and Knowledge be the Stability of your Times, and the Fear of the Lord your Treasure. *Amen.*

The Lord make your Days many, your Reign prosperous, your Fleets and Armies victorious; and may you be reverenced and beloved by all your Subjects, and ever increase in Favour with God and man. *Amen.*

The glorious Majesty of the Lord our God be upon you : may he bless you with all temporal and spiritual Happiness in this world, and crown you with Glory and Immortality in the world to come. *Amen.*

Then the Archbishop turneth to the People, and saith :

AND the same Lord God Almighty grant that the Clergy and Nobles assembled here for this great and solemn Service, and together with them all the People of the Land, fearing God, and honouring the King, may by the merciful Superintendency of the Divine Providence, and the vigilant Care of our gracious Sovereign, continually enjoy Peace, Plenty, and Prosperity, through Jesus Christ our Lord, to whom, with the Eternal Father, and God the Holy Ghost, be Glory in the Church world without end. *Amen.*

Then the Choir begins to sing the *Te Deum*, and the King goes to the Chair on which His Majesty first sate on the East Side of the Throne, the Two Bishops His Supporters, the Great Officers, and other Peers, attending Him, every one in his place, the two Swords being carried before Him, and there reposes Himself.

Te Deum.

WE praise Thee, O God ; &c

Form and Order of the Service

SECT. XV.

The Inthronization.

The *Te Deum* being ended, the King will ascend the Theatre, and be lifted up into His Throne by the Archbishop and Bishops, and other Peers of the Kingdom, and being *Inthronized*, or placed therein, all the *Great Officers*, Those that bear the *Swords* and the *Sceptres*, and the rest of the *Nobles*, stand round about the steps of the Throne, and the Archbishop standing before the King, saith:

STAND firm, and hold fast from henceforth the Seat and State of Royal and Imperial Dignity which is this day delivered unto you in the Name, and by the Authority of Almighty God, and by the Hands of Us the Bishops and Servants of God, though unworthy: And as you see Us to approach nearer to God's Altar, so vouchsafe the more graciously to continue to Us your Royal Favour and Protection. And the Lord God Almighty, whose Ministers we are, and the Stewards of his Mysteries, establish your Throne in Righteousness, that it may stand fast for evermore, like as the Sun before him, and as the faithful Witness in Heaven. *Amen.*

SECT. XVI.

The Homage.

The Exhortation being ended, all the Peers then present do their Homage publickly and solemnly unto the King upon the Theatre, and in the mean time the Treasurer of the Household throws among the People Medals of Gold and Silver, as the King's Princely Largess or Donative.

The Archbishop first kneels down before His Majesty's Knees, and the rest of the Bishops kneel on either Hand and

283

The Coronation of Edward VII

about Him ; and they do their Homage together, for the shortening of the Ceremony, the Archbishop saying :

I *M.* Archbishop of *Canterbury* [*And so every one of the rest,* I *N.* Bishop of *N., repeating the rest audibly after the Archbishop*] will be faithful and true, and Faith and Truth will bear, unto you our Sovereign Lord, and your Heirs, Kings or Queens of the United Kingdom of *Great Britain* and *Ireland.* And I will do, and truly acknowledge the Service of the Lands which I claim to hold of you, as in right of the Church.   So help me God.

Then the Archbishop kisseth the King's Hand, and so the rest of the Bishops present after him.

After which the other Peers of the Realm do their Homage in like manner, the Dukes first by themselves, and so the Marquesses, the Earls, the Viscounts, and the Barons, severally ; the first of each Order kneeling before His Majesty, and the rest with and about him all putting off their Coronets, and the first of each class beginning, and the rest saying after him :

I *N.* Duke, or Earl, &c., of *N.* do become your Liege man of Life and Limb, and of earthly worship, and Faith and Truth I will bear unto you, to live and die, against all manner of Folks.   So help me God.

(*Note,* That Copies of this Homage must be provided by the Heralds for every Class of the Nobility.)

The Peers having done their Homage, stand all together round about the King ; and each Class or Degree going by themselves, or (as it was at the Coronation of King *Charles* the First and Second) every Peer one by one, in Order, putting off their Coronets, singly ascend the Throne again, and stretching forth their hands, do touch the Crown on His

Form and Order of the Service

Majesty's Head, as promising by that Ceremony to be ever ready to support it with all their power, and then every one of them kisseth the King's Hand.

While the Peers are thus doing their Homage, and the Medals thus thrown about, the King, if He thinks good, delivers His *Sceptre* with the *Cross* to the Lord of the Manour of *Worksop*, to hold ; and the other *Sceptre*, or *Rod*, with the *Dove*, to the Lord that carried it in the Procession.

And the Bishops that support the King in the Procession may also ease Him by supporting the Crown, as there shall be occasion.

During the Performance of the Homage the Choir sing this

ANTHEM.

THIS is the day which the Lord hath made, we will rejoice and be glad in it.

Lord, grant the King a long life : that His years may endure throughout all generations.

He shall dwell before God for ever: O prepare thy loving mercy and faithfulness, that they may preserve Him.

Blessed be the Lord Thy God, who delighteth in Thee to set Thee on the Throne.

When the Homage is ended, the Drums beat, and the Trumpets sound, and all the People shout, crying out,

God save King EDWARD.

Long live King EDWARD.

May the King live for ever.

The Solemnity of the *Coronation* being thus ended, the Archbishop leaves the King in His Throne, and goes down to the Altar.

The Coronation of Edward VII

SECT. XVII.

The Communion.

Then the Offertory begins, the Archbishop reading these
Sentences :

LET your light so shine before men, &c.

The King descends from His Throne, attended by His
Supporters, and assisted by the Lord Great Chamberlain,
the Sword of State being carried before Him, and goes
to the Steps of the Altar, where taking off His Crown,
which He delivers to the Lord Great Chamberlain to hold,
He kneels down.

And first the *King* offers *Bread* and *Wine* for the Communion,
which being brought out of King *Edward's* Chapel, and
delivered into His Hands, the *Bread* upon the *Paten* by
the *Bishop* that read the *Epistle*, and the *Wine* in the
Chalice by the *Bishop* that read the *Gospel*, are by the
Archbishop received from the King, and reverently placed
upon the Altar, and decently covered with a fair linen
Cloth, the Archbishop first saying this Prayer :

BLESS, O Lord, we beseech thee, these thy Gifts, and
sanctify them unto this holy use, that by them we may
be made partakers of the Body and Blood of thine only
begotten Son Jesus Christ, and fed unto everlasting life
of Soul and Body : And that thy Servant King EDWARD
may be enabled to the discharge of His weighty Office,
whereunto of thy great goodness thou hast called and
appointed Him. Grant this, O Lord, for Jesus Christ's
sake, our only Mediator and Advocate. *Amen.*

Then the King kneeling, as before, makes His second Oblation,
a *Purse of Gold*, which the *Treasurer* of the *Household*
delivers to the *Lord Great Chamberlain*, and he to *His*

286

Form and Order of the Service

Majesty. And the Archbishop coming to Him, receives it into the Bason, and placeth it upon the Altar.

After which the Archbishop says,

O God, who dwellest in the high and holy place, with them also who are of an humble spirit; Look down mercifully upon this thy Servant EDWARD our King, here humbling Himself before Thee at thy Footstool; and graciously receive these *Oblations*, which in humble acknowledgment of thy Sovereignty over all, and of thy great Bounty to Him in particular, He has now offered up unto thee, through Jesus Christ, our only Mediator and Advocate. *Amen.*

Then the *King* goes to His *Chair* on the South Side of the Altar, and kneeling down at His Faldstool, the Archbishop saith :

Let us pray for the whole state of Christ's Church militant here in earth.

ALMIGHTY and everliving God, &c.

The Exhortation.

YE that do truly, &c.

The general Confession.

ALMIGHTY God, Father of our Lord Jesus Christ, &c.

The Absolution.

ALMIGHTY God our heavenly Father, &c.

After which shall be said,

Hear what comfortable words our Saviour Christ saith unto all that truly turn to him.

COME unto me, &c.

287

The Coronation of Edward VII

After which the Archbishop shall proceed, saying,

Archb. Lift up your hearts.

Answ. *We lift them up unto the Lord.*

Archb. Let us give thanks unto our Lord God.

Answ. *It is meet and right so to do.*

Then shall the Archbishop turn to the Lord's Table, and say,

IT is very meet, right, and our bounden duty that we should at all times, and in all places, give thanks unto thee, O Lord, Holy Father, Almighty, Everlasting God :

WHO hast at this time given us thy Servant our Sovereign King EDWARD to be the Defender of thy Faith, and the Protector of thy People ; that under Him we may lead a quiet and peaceable life in all Godliness and Honesty.

THEREFORE with Angels and Archangels, &c.

The Prayer of Address.

WE do not presume to come to this thy Table, &c.

The Prayer of Consecration.

ALMIGHTY God, our heavenly Father, &c.

When the *Archbishop*, and *Dean* of *Westminster*, with the *Bishops Assistants*, namely, the *Preacher*, and those who *read the Litany*, and the *Epistle and Gospel*, have communicated in both kinds, the King advances to the Altar, and kneels down, and the Archbishop shall administer the Bread, and the Dean of *Westminster* the Cup, to Him.

Form and Order of the Service

At the Delivery of the Bread shall be said,

THE Body of our Lord Jesus Christ, &c.

At the Delivery of the Cup,

THE Blood of our Lord Jesus Christ, &c.

The King then puts on His Crown, and taking the Sceptres in His Hands, again, repairs to His Throne.

Then the *Archbishop* goeth on to the *Post-Communion*, saying,

OUR Father, &c.

Then this Prayer.

O LORD and heavenly Father, &c.

Then shall be said,

GLORY be to God on high, &c.

The Choir then sing the following anthem :

ANTHEM.

HALLELUJAH : For the Lord God Omnipotent reigneth. The kingdom of this World is become the kingdom of our Lord, and of his Christ. And he shall reign for ever and ever, King of Kings, and Lord of Lords. Hallelujah.

After the Anthem the Archbishop reads the final Prayers.

SECT. XVIII.

The final Prayers.

ASSIST us mercifully, O Lord, &c.

289

The Coronation of Edward VII

SECT. XIX.

The Recess.

THE whole Coronation Office being thus performed, the *King* attended and accompanied as before, the four Swords being carried before Him, descends from His Throne Crowned, and carrying His *Sceptre* and *Rod* in His Hands, goes into the Area Eastward of the Theatre, and passes on through the Door on the *South side* of the *Altar* into King *Edward's Chapel;* and as He passes by the Altar, the rest of the *Regalia* lying upon it, are to be delivered by the *Dean* of *Westminster* to the Lords that carried them in the Procession, and so they proceed in State into the Chapel, the Organ and other Instruments all the while playing.

The *King* being come into the Chapel, and standing before the *Altar*, will deliver the *Sceptre* with the *Dove* to the *Archbishop*, who will lay it upon the Altar there. The *King* will then be disrobed of His *Imperial Mantle*, and arrayed in His *Royal Robe* of *Purple Velvet* by the Lord Great Chamberlain.

The *Archbishop*, being still vested in his Cope, will then place the *Orb* in His Majesty's Left Hand. And the *Gold Spurs* and *King Edward's Staff* are given into the hands of the Dean of *Westminster*, and by him laid upon the Altar. Which being done, the *Archbishop* and *Bishops* will divest themselves of their Copes, and leave them there, proceeding in their usual Habits.

Then His Majesty will proceed through the Choir to the West Door of the Abbey, in the same manner as He came, wearing His *Crown*, and bearing in His Right Hand the *Sceptre* with the *Cross*, and in His Left the *Orb;* all *Peers* wearing their Coronets, and the *Archbishops* and *Bishops* their Caps.

CPSIA information can be obtained at www.ICGtesting.com
Printed in the USA
LVOW08s1113151013

356987LV00002B/356/P